Some of the names of people and places have been [changed to] protect
the privacy of those ind

MW01232650

No part of this publicatio
system, or transmitted in any form or by any means- electronic,
mechanical, photocopy, recording, or any other way, without the prior
permission of the author or publisher. All rights reserved.

From a Gang to God

Introduction

This book is about the life of Ronald Renee Baldridge, bka "Lizard". This
book is dedicated to my mother, Earline "Doll" Motton Baldridge, to whom
I owe everything. Her undying love and commitment to raising two sons is
beyond exceptional. She set an example for me and taught me a lesson
in compassion, especially when it comes to little children, the elderly, and
hurting people. Thank you momma for teaching me to speak up for my
beliefs, for raising two sons on your own, and never giving up on us . To
my brother, Darryl: Thank you for all your prayers and for being there for
me when I was hurting. I wouldn't trade you for another brother in this
world. To Lieutenant Steve Grisham: I thank you for being a friend and
brother in Christ. Thank you for your obedience to reach out to me when
others were afraid to. To Candy and family, Jeanne and family, Mary
Martha and family, and Phee and family: You are the best sisters a man
could ask for. I would like to thank both of my aunts Girlie and Mary Ann
for their love, advice, and support through trials and tribulations. Melvin
Carter, Steve, Michael, Tony, Mervyn, Sonny, Mr. C. Nelson and Alex
thanks for your friendship family. To Jeffrey Taylor: Thank you for helping
me write this book and for being a good friend. To all my family at

Melanie's Restaurant, I love you, the support and the wonderful food. I would like to thank all individuals whom I consider friends and family. I would not want my life to change in any direction because I recognize that one turn away from the path my life has taken thus far would have robbed me of the opportunity to cross paths with the individuals I consider family and friends. . I'd like to thank the staff at The Regional Medical Center for your awesome work you do. Finally, I want to thank the two unsung Heroes Paramedics who worked on me and drove without haste to The Regional Medical Center (The Med).

This is a story about a man who has survived being shot five different times, 24 different operations. Additionally, this same man has broken his left ankle, left hand, and right leg. For the past 16 years he has lived with a dislocated right hip, and has survived being thrown from a car that was traveling 45 miles per hour 3 feet in the air . This young man lives in constant chronic back pain.

What would you say if I told you that this man was a former gang banger, who at one time hated police officers and white people, only to eventually be baptized by a white police officer? Would you say this man has been through a lot? Perhaps you would feel sorry for the man. The following pages describe in detail how all of the above came about.

FROM A GANG TO GOD

©

The Beginning JOURNEY
Clarksdale, Mississippi

1929

In 1929, Kizzie Motton gave birth to a beautiful baby dark skinned girl. This baby was so precious; she looked like a pretty little doll. Thus, she was given the nickname of Doll, and was referred to as such by family and close friends. Her very first sounds were of sorrow; the shedding of tears, and from a smack on the butt. That would be the first of many tears that would be shed over hardship, pain, racism, and prejudice.

Now Kizzie Motton did not have time to raise any of her children like she desired. Her brothers and sisters did not know what to do to help her while she suffered. She wanted a life for herself but she became extremely ill to the point she died. So, all of Kizzie's children went to live with their grandmother and aunties. Earline, bka "Doll", was one of three girls. Doll was a beautiful black girl, with smooth mahogany skin that looked a lot like satin, a smile that could light up any room, and soft curly hair, Doll looked like an expensive china doll.

Ann was the middle child of the three girls. Doll was the baby. Ann and Doll went to live with their grandmother. Girlie, the oldest of the three girls, went to live with her auntie.

Ann was very protective of her baby sister. Both Ann and Doll were abused harshly, both physically and emotionally. Sometimes these girls were beaten with fire logs across their backs and verbally abused. This type of abuse would cause Doll to become hard and often misunderstood later in life.

There were many nights that the girls went to bed hungry. Often times they would share food with each other. There was no counseling for these girls, so often times they had to rely on each other for counseling and comforting.

The two girls were raised in a time when African Americans were looked upon as being less than human. They saw a lot in their days growing up. They saw black women being raped by white men who would get away with it. They also saw Black men run for their lives from angry mobs of white men. There was no real justice for them. Many black men and women chose to fight back by becoming educated and learning their rights. They had no way of knowing back then that one day, not only would black men whistle openly at white women, but they would marry them, have children by them, and walk down the street in broad day light hand-in-hand with them.

It was very difficult for a little girl to see that kind of fear in a black man's eyes. However, these experiences are what would build Doll and her sisters into the phenomenal women they would become.

Surviving in the South as a young, poor, black woman in the 1930's and 1940's was more than a notion. Not only did she have to fight against racism and prejudice, but also Doll had to learn how to stay alive from day to day. All Doll and her sister had on their grandmother's farm to stay alive was a cow, a pig, and a few chickens. Doll spent her days learning how to do things many women today would never be able to endure. Duties such as slaughtering hogs, picking cotton and butchering cows were common practice for Doll and her sister Ann.

Doll spent most of her days picking cotton, going to school, and playing. Now Doll did not mind going to school. She was a bright little girl that excelled in her studies. Every morning she would walk with her lunch bucket in hand on her way to school in what little clothes she had.

Education was important to Doll and her sister. However, survival was present and staring her and her sister Ann in the face. Eventually, both girls were forced to drop out of school to work on the farm and pick cotton to survive. They did whatever they had to do to live then or to survive with the thought it has to get better, if not for them at least for their children in the future.

Doll often had to fight other women and men. In those days, men liked younger women. Some of these older men thought they were going to disrespect Doll in public while she was out enjoying herself. These men did not seem to understand what the word no meant. One man in particular tried to get rough with Doll in a cafe. Little did he know Doll's Uncle Isaac was watching from a distance? Now Uncle Isaac was very protective of his little nieces. Naturally, he had to step in when he saw how his niece was being treated. Grabbing the harasser from behind, pulling his shirt over his head and driving several punches to the face, along with a kick in the side, Uncle Isaac delivered some old school jacking. Needless to say, that pursuer never bothered Doll again.

Uncle Isaac Simmons was always there for his niece. He was the only uncle who remained behind in Mississippi. The other two had gone up north to pursue a better life. One Albert Simmons moved to Chicago and opened up a couple stores, and Richard Simmons who moved to New York and started a family.

However, the harassment did not stop with men. There were often women that wanted to disrespect Doll. One night, in Clarksdale, Mississippi, Doll encountered a young woman who thought she was going to disrespect Doll and her older sister. Doll was not having it. Doll politely walked up to the woman while the woman was talking about what she was going to do to Doll and her sister. Before the woman knew it, Doll had cut the woman with a straight blade. Blood shot out of the woman's arm. The family had to smuggle Doll out of town because the police were looking for her.

Now Doll was a beautiful petite woman who was 5'7" tall and 130lbs. Yet, she was full of strength, grace, and energy. She was a vibrant woman that loved life and boldness. She was not afraid to speak her mind or fight. She basically taught herself how to survive on her own in the city streets of Clarksdale, Dobbs, Greenville, and other small towns in Mississippi. Things that would make a normal woman cry, made Doll stronger.

Doll lived through the World War II, Viet Nam, and the Civil Rights Movement. Growing up in the Mississippi Delta, Doll understood first hand the struggles of African Americans. She was an active participant in the Civil Rights Movement. She participated in several marches, sit-ins, and protests. Earline and other protesters riding buses with their heads down and the lights out traveling down dark roads possibly filled with white men in white hoods. Participating in peaceful sit in protests. Doll was afraid of nothing.

The Greenville Years

Greenville, Mississippi

1957

By the time Doll became a young woman, she was pretty good at picking bags of cotton. That was not the only kind of work she could find as a young lady in the 1950's. Doll worked hard picking cotton, working odd jobs and was able to save money. Unlike a lot of the girls Doll grew up with, Doll did not have any kids. She was a free spirit and wanted to travel and see the world.

Ever since she was a little girl, she had a great desire to see the World. Despite the fact she had never been outside the state of Mississippi, she knew the world had more to offer than manual labor in the hot Mississippi Delta sun.

So, she used the money she had set aside from picking cotton, working odd jobs and began to travel. New York, Chicago, Georgia, Memphis, Texas, and Indiana were just a few of the many places she visited during her years as a young woman.

Doll always dressed to impress when she stepped into a city where her family was. Adorned in the finest silk, satins, and furs, Doll looked like a million bucks. Additionally, she wore expensive jewelry that made her look like a queen. There is no doubt about it; this Mississippi lady had class and style.

One hot summer day, Doll decided to go for a drive. She couldn't know that on that day she would have a close call with death.

As she traveled down a local highway, she collided with another driver who disregarded a stop sign. The other vehicle collided with Doll on her passenger side, spraying glass everywhere.

Doll's face was damaged severely from cuts caused by the glass. Blood was all over the scene of the accident. Earline was in shock as the medics and police drove fast through the streets to the hospital. This beautiful doll could not believe what had happened. Her face was so badly damaged that plastic surgery was required.

She could not get the vision of the accident out of her mind. She would often wake up in the middle of the night screaming and with night sweats because of a nightmare she had about this wreck. Needless to say, she did not get much rest during this time.

For weeks on end, she attempted to get up the nerve to look at the damage that was caused to her face. She prayed to God and asked Him to calm her nerves and give her the strength she would need to endure this situation.

The day finally came when the bandages would be removed. Doll was a nervous wreck and had tears flowing down her face. The doctor gave her something to calm her nerves. She was scared to death. She had this horrible feeling that she was going to be severely disfigured for the rest of her human life.

One by one, the bandages were removed. Doll looked anxiously at the expression on the doctor's face in an attempt to read his reaction and judge if the surgery had been a success. However, the doctor maintained a neutral expression. No indication was given. Her anxiety grew as each bandage was removed. To Doll, it seemed as if time was going in slow motion.

Finally, the moment came when Doll could look in the mirror. Tears of joy flowed down her face as she saw the face she recognized as her own looking back at her. The doctors had done an excellent job. Her face was not damaged at all.

Doll's children would get the chance to see that big beautiful smile of hers. However, one thing did change permanently as a result of the accident. From that time on she had a fear of driving, and she never drove again.

John D. Baldridge
Greenville, Mississippi
1963

Ann was Doll's sister who lived in Greenville. Together, Ann and Doll gave each other the support the two women needed at that time. Now Ann had three children Eric, Demetria , Maxine and Doll spoiled them each chance she got. Many times Ann and her daughter Demetria would argue about everything from chores to friends. Whenever these arguments broke out, Demetria would run off to her auntie Doll. All of Ann's children were crazy about their auntie.

Now Girlie, Doll's older other sister of the three, eventually left Dobbs, Mississippi which was a small town on the outskirts of Clarksdale, to relocate 60 miles north in Memphis, Tennessee. However, that distance did not keep Doll from visiting her sister. Doll would ride up to Memphis in a heartbeat to visit her sister. Every time Doll traveled to visit relatives in distant cities, she was always dressed from head to toe in the finest furs, silks, and jewelry. Doll truly lived up to her name, for she looked like a living Doll.

Now Doll was not only close to Ann's children. She also adored Girlie's children. One afternoon, shortly after arriving in Memphis coming from Greenville, Doll hit the streets to find one of her nephew's, Junior. Doll suspected she would find him on Beale Street and she was correct.

Doll found Junior, a.k.a. Bow Legs, on the side walk drunk as a skunk. Bow Legs had recently developed a serious drinking problem and Doll was very concerned about him. Doll loved her some Bow Legs.

Doll would often get a room and take Bow Legs to that room so he could sober up. While he was sobering up, she would sit there and talk with him about his drinking problem. She knew he was killing himself slowly, and Junior knew it also. However, he did not care and did not feel anyone else cared at that time. Doll eventually got Bow Legs to promise he would try to stop drinking. Bow legs did eventually keep his promise to his auntie and was able to remain sober. He came to realize that his entire family cared a great deal for him. That was many countless nights of prayers answered by God for his mother.

Doll did not have to say that she cared for her family. Her actions showed it and spoke much louder than any words. However, Doll eventually wanted to share her love with her own. Doll's own motherly instinct began to beckon and call her to be a mother. Doll was getting tired of only caring and spoiling her nieces, nephews and other people's children. She wanted to have some children of her own. It was at this time that Doll began to consider settling down and starting a family; something that would have been completely out of the question just a few years ago.

One afternoon, a tall dark-skinned man walked into Doll's life. He introduced himself as John D. Baldridge, b.k.a. J.D. On April 5, 1963, Doll became Mrs. John D. Baldridge. John loved his new wife very much and he was a very good provider. He worked hard and provided her with a nice home on Eureka Street in Greenville. Eventually, Doll became pregnant with her first child. The couple was very happy.

No one could believe that Doll had settled down and gotten married. When Doll turned up expecting a child, the family was really dismayed. It was difficult to believe that the once world traveler who was a bit on the wild side had actually settled into the roll as a housewife. Now even though Doll was now a wife and expecting mother, she did continue to travel. This worried her sisters and other relatives, but they knew that when Doll had her mind made up there was no convincing her otherwise. Needless to say Doll continued to travel with her first child inside her.

Two Black Pearls

Darryl Fitzgerald Baldridge

Greenville, Mississippi

1965

On August 1, 1965, a beautiful, black baby boy was born. The heat was stifling that afternoon when Darryl Fitzgerald Baldridge was born. He was named after President Kennedy, who had died due to an assassin's bullet just two years earlier. Finally, all the long nights with upset stomachs, swollen ankles, mood swings and cravings for strange foods paid off. It was worth it to Doll just to hear the cry of the very first child to which she had given birth. The pain was but a small challenge for her to lay eyes on her beautiful, black baby boy. She finally had a baby of her own that she could spoil. Doll bought Darryl all types of little baby clothes and buddies. She dressed him up in his little shirt and pants and would take him to the park.

Everyone in the family adored Darryl and the whole family pitched in to take care of him. Some of Doll's nieces would often baby-sit for him. Demetria was one of those nieces who in particular loved spending time with baby Darryl. Demetria would carry him all over the city of Greenville, visiting different people and attending this function and that function. Demetria and Maxine spent so much time with Darryl that people often thought Darryl was her baby.

In those days, Nelson Street was the place to be in Greenville. Nelson Street had nightclubs, restaurants, beauty parlors, barber shops, an ice cream parlor, and a drug store. Nelson Street was the Harlem of the Delta. Mr. Baldridge's family lived near Nelson Street. Many times J. D.'s mother, Darryl's grandmother, would come and baby-sit Darryl, despite the fact that she did not get along with Doll. Many times these women would argue. Darryl's grandmother even expressed doubt as to whether her son played a role in the fathering of Darryl.

Darryl was curious about everything, even those things that were dangerous to him. One day Darryl became curious about what was on the stove. Fire was pretty to him. His mother clearly told him not to touch the pot on the stove. However, Darryl waited until his mother was in the other room. Suddenly Doll heard a loud scream ring out from the kitchen. Darryl had gotten close to the pot on the stove and touched it. It burned him badly. She quickly picked him up and carried him to the doctor who gave her some ointments to place on the burns and soothe the pain. From that point on J. D. and Doll were extremely cautious and watched his every move.

As time passed by Doll eventually began working for a woman on Nelson Street. Demetria watched Darryl while Doll was at work. That worked out well for everyone involved except Demetria who would miss school every once in a while. Doll continued to travel some, taking Darryl on trips with her to Chicago, New Orleans, and particularly Memphis, Tennessee to visit Darryl's other auntie. All the family was crazy about Darryl. Darryl was surrounded by lots of love and developed well in this nurturing environment.

HOMETOWN GROWING UP
Ronald Renee Baldridge
Greenville, Mississippi
1967
The days turned into months and the months into years. Life in the Baldridge family did not change much. Doll continued to work for the woman on Nelson Street, J. D. continued to work hard and provide for his wife and son, Demetria continued to watch Darryl while the eldest Baldridge's were at work. Doll continued to travel from time to time to visit relatives. She always had her baby at her side wherever she traveled.

Two summers after Darryl was born, Doll found herself pregnant again. She hoped so much that she would have a baby-girl. She wanted very badly to have a little version of herself; someone with whom she could play dress-up and have tea. However, fate had other plans. On August

15

12, 1967, Doll gave birth to another beautiful baby boy. This baby was bright red, and even though she was hoping for a baby girl, he was born a boy. She gave him the middle name of Renee.

Ronald Renee Baldridge was indeed a beautiful baby boy, just like his brother, just lighter. However, he had asthma. J. D. and Doll had no idea that the effects of their smoking would have such a traumatic impact on the health of their baby boy. After all, Darryl had no health impairments of any kind.

Doll tried multiple methods to help her baby boy, both conventional and non-conventional methods. She tried everything from vaporizers, prayer, and teas with caffeine in them. Nothing seemed to work other than conventional medicine. There were countless nights of staying up with little Ronald.

Complicating matters was the fact that Ronald was allergic to everything. He was allergic to pollen, eggs, dust mites, flowers, cigarette smoke, pets of all kinds, and even certain types of medicines. Throughout his childhood Ronald had to be careful not to run too much or play to hard. Additionally, Ronald had to keep his inhaler in his possession at all times. Medicines such as Theophyline and Inhalers he would later have to take in life.

Now Darryl was very excited about having a baby brother. One afternoon when Doll was standing at the stove in the kitchen cooking dinner and baby Ronald was in his baby rocker, Darryl ran into the kitchen. He looked at baby Ronald and looked at his momma and said "baby momma, my baby brother". Doll looked at Darryl and said, "yes, Darryl, that is your baby brother". He took his bottle out of his mouth and put it in his brother's mouth. Darryl never drank from a bottle again. Ronald cherished that bottle for years to come.

At first, Ronald could not say his brother's name Gerald. So, he called him yield. It did not matter to Doll; in fact she thought it was cute. Doll was very protective of her baby boys. Some people thought Doll was too protective. She would sit at their bedsides and read them stories from the Bible and watch them as they fell into dreamland. She would often continue to sit on the sides of their beds and watch them sleep; making sure mosquitoes and spiders did not bite them. This was a practice she would continue until her boys were well into their 20's. Darryl would wind up the rocker and watch his little brother's face change with laughter.

On Their Own in Greenville

Greenville, Mississippi

1968

Doll and J. D. split up shortly after Ronald was born. They had differences that they could not resolve. So, Mr. J. D. Baldridge disappeared from the lives of his wife and kids and they never saw him again. This put a strain on the Baldridge finances. Doll had to work two jobs just to help ends meet. She worked for Dan's Bar B Que and also worked as a nanny for the Atkins family. Mr. and Mrs. Atkins were attorneys who were God-fearing and loved Doll and her two sons like they were their own flesh and blood. They had two children; a boy and a girl. At bedtime, Doll would fix all of the kids hot chocolate and have them say their bedtime prayers. Then she would tuck them all under the covers in the same bed and off to sleep they went until it was time for Doll to get off work.

Having no one to watch the boys at times, Doll often had to take them with her when she ran her errands. She would take them to the grocery store, to the beauty shop, and anywhere else she needed to go unless her nephew or niece's would baby-sit them. She was very proud of her boys, even though she had initially hoped for at least one little girl. She soon discovered that raising boys could be just as fun and satisfying as raising girls. She loved to dress her two little boys up in their Sunday suits and take them to church. The sisters would get the families together and have dinner on Sundays after church. She was indeed a very proud mother. It was a weekly thing where Doll and Ann would get together and go out to party, it never failed they'd end up auguring by the time they got home, but they really loved each other.

One day in April of 1968, during one of Doll's routine trips to the beauty shop to get her hair fixed. Ronald was in his mother arms, while Darryl was sitting on the floor playing. The radio was on while the women talked. A voice interrupted the music with some very bad news across the airways. It was April 6, 1968, to be exact and Dr. Martin Luther King, Jr. had just been shot by an assassin's bullet at the Lorraine Motel in Memphis, Tennessee. Everyone in the beauty shop suddenly got quiet. No one said a word. All that could be heard were the sounds of women sobbing. No one could believe that any one would want to hurt the man who wanted only, peace, equal justice, civil rights, and respect for all humanity. Doll held her sons close. Her two boys were too young to fully understand what had taken place, but they knew by the reactions of the women in that beauty shop that it must have been pretty terrible. Doll explained to them that a very bad thing had happened to a very good man. Darryl and Ronald would never forget those sobbing women in the beauty shop on that day.

Life in Greenville was fun and full of happy memories for the Baldridge children. They were surrounded by people who loved and cared for them. Some of them were blood relatives, but many of them were not. Regardless, Darryl and Ronald knew they were loved. Their mother would often play board games with them before bed and say prayers with them. Then she would sit on the side of their bed and watch them for many hours into the night. Sometimes their Tee -Tee as they called her would sometimes come and get them to go fishing. Ronald hated the smell of fish but loved hanging out with Tee-Tee.

Now the children in the neighborhood had no problem creating ways to entertain themselves. In those days children had imaginations and they used their imaginations to keep themselves entertained efficiently and effectively. One of their favorite games consisted of seeing who could pick up baby Ronald without being hit. Ronald played the game with joy. He loved popping those kids up side their heads with his bottle that his big brother gave to him. He would laugh every time he popped one of them. Even though he was only a baby, it was clear to all who observed this game that baby Ronald definitely understood the object of this game. The funny part was he never hit his big brother. He knew his big brother loved him very much.

Time passed and the boys began to grow up. Ronald was a character. There was no doubt about that. Doll had a friend named Barbara. Barbara had two little girls. One was named Patricia and the other was named Nooke. One afternoon, Barbara came over to pick Doll and her two sons up. Ronald liked Patricia and decided he would show her. He leaned over and planted a kiss on Patricia's right cheek. In return, he received a hard right across the jaw. The swing made such a loud thud that even their mother's heard it. Darryl could not help but laugh at his baby brother because Ronald's face turned red.

Several weeks later on Eureka Street Darryl, Ronald, and a pretty little girl from around the corner were playing kick ball over at Uncle Jesse's and Aunt Savanna's house; some neighbors that treated Doll and her sons as if they were blood-relatives. At one point, the ball went into the streets after it was kicked. The little girl told him to go after the ball. Darryl told his brother not to go into the streets for the ball. However, Ronald didn't listen and went anyway. Before he knew it a car came from nowhere and smacked him. Their mother was at work and had no idea what had happened to her baby son.

Blood was coming out of his nose, mouth, and ears. Darryl stood crying calling his little brother's name. Aunt Savannah came out in a panic. Someone must have called emergency services because suddenly they heard an ambulance and a sheriff car pull up. The driver explained that he did not see him until it was too late to stop. A crowd of people came out of nowhere to see little Ronald lay in the streets bleeding from his nose, mouth, and ears. The paramedics picked Ronald up and put him on the stretcher to take him to General Hospital. Darryl remained at Aunt Savannah and Uncle Jesse's house. Their auntie, Ann, and her children stood by outside praying and hoping their little nephew and cousin would be okay.

His big brother Darryl was scared for him but he would try to remain strong for his little brother after all, being strong was all he knew. They were a team, is what their mother always told them. They had to remain strong when times were tough. From what Darryl could see, these were tough times if ever there were tough times.

Doll was notified that her baby was hurt in an accident. She immediately left her job and headed straight for General Hospital. With tears in her eyes and praying a mile a minute. She arrived at the hospital and asked the nurse at the front desk where her baby was. One of the nurses on duty showed her what room to go into. The doctors and nurses were extremely nervous because he was doing something they weren't familiar with .The doctor, nurses, and, Earline was in the room watching little Ronald rock himself back and forth to sleep. Earline had to explain to the doctors that was his way of going to sleep. The doctors and nurses thought he was having a seizure or something. Mary prayers had been answered that day for her little nephew.

The Next couple of weeks Ronald was back up and at it again. He was a tough little boy. One of the fears the doctors had was that the accident would trigger his Asthma. However, it never flared up during the recovery process. Not long after the accident the Baldridge family moved from Eureka Street to Gloster Street. Once they were settled in their new home, Doll gave her sons a turtle to help them feel better and forget about the car incident. The boys were excited to have an additional member to the family. However, just like their father that turtle eventually crawled out the window and they never saw it again. Wherever Doll went, her boys were near. One afternoon, Doll went to the grocery store. As always, her boys were with her. She instructed them to stay beside each other in the store at all times and hold hands. Doll had stepped over to another aisle when suddenly a loud cry rang out. It was the cry of one of her sons. Doll rushed around the corner to find Darryl picking his crying baby brother up off the ground.

She asked Darryl, who was only five years old, what had happened. Darryl explained that he was standing there with his brother like he was told and a woman came rushing down the aisle and pushed him down. Ronald was only three years old at this time. Doll asked Darryl if he could point out the woman who had done this horrible thing. Darryl thought he probably could easily identify this woman. It was difficult for Doll to imagine who would do such a cruel thing to a child. The thought both hurt Doll and made her angry.

Doll and her two sons started walking the aisles of the grocery store, searching for the criminal who had dared to mess with her baby boy. Suddenly, Darryl spotted the woman. Doll walked over and politely introduced herself. She asked the woman why she pushed her son down without bothering to pick him up. The woman replied that he shouldn't have been in the way. That was the wrong response. Doll began to feel herself tremble all over with both sorrow and anger. After all, Ronald was not only her baby; he was sickly on top of everything else. How could anyone knocked down a sickly baby and keep on moving like nothing had happened?

Before Doll knew what had happened, she hit the woman. She was about to cut the woman when the store manager intervened. The manager took Doll's story and notified the authorities. The woman was charged with battery on a minor.

1971 was the year Darryl began first grade. He attended elementary school down the streets and across the railroad tracks. It was just a few blocks up the streets from their house. Ronald knew instinctively approximately what time Darryl got home from school and he would come out to the porch at the same time every day and watch for his big brother to come across the tracks. One hot summer day in June around 2:50 p.m. Ronald came outside to sit on the porch, as was the routine. Ronald saw some boys following his brother and pushing him. Darryl dropped one of his books and tried to pick it up. In no time at all, Ronald jumped off the porch and ran across the tracks to help his brother. With a rock to the head of one of the bullies and a punch in the stomach to another one, little Ronald fought those two little boys. Darryl however didn't stick around long enough to find out what happened. He ran to the house to tell his mom. In what seemed like no time, Doll rushed out of the house, with Darryl in her hands, up the tracks to retrieve Ronald. However, by the time she reached Ronald he was coming across the tracks dusting him off, successful in his first fight. There would be plenty more times in the future for Darryl to redeem himself. Doll told her sons never to run off and leave each other in a fight. Darryl for one never forgot those words. No one had any way of knowing that fighting would some day be a regular way of life, a necessity, for Ronald.

Time passed and the boys got bigger. Ronald continued to have problems with asthma. . She tried everything from having him spit into the mouths of frogs in an attempt to transfer the asthma onto the frog, putting him under a tree limb and nailing a nail over his head into the tree. Doll continued to work hard to keep food and shelter for her and her boys.

Earline "Doll" Baldridge was a survivalist; a strong black woman who was determined to teach her sons who to survive themselves. She knew the world was a tough place and she did not want life for her two boys to be as rough as it had been for her. She was the type of mother she wished she had growing up. She was the selfless kind of mother; the kind of mother that sacrificed herself and her own needs and wants to see that her children have a rich childhood. That's what a man and woman are supposed to do that's parents. They are supposed to stop living their dreams and aspirations to help their children pursue theirs.

Doll was very resourceful when it came to her boys. Even though times were tough financially, she always found a way to spoil them with gifts for their birthdays and at Christmas. She often went without meat herself so that her two boys could have meat in their diet. She would sacrifice her own sleep to sit by their bedsides and make sure nothing was biting them. She never regretted the sacrifices that she made as a mother. Hearing the laughter from her two boys and seeing joy in their eyes was reassurance that she had done a good job as a mother.

The holidays in Greenville were very special, especially Christmas time. Doll always saved up enough money to buy her sons what they wanted. She would have her boys write down all the gifts they wanted and they would hang the list on the wall in stockings. Cousin Eric, one of Doll's nephews, played Santa Claus and Doll cooked sweet potato pies, cakes, turkey dressing, spaghetti, greens, macaroni and cheese, and all the other foods that make a Christmas meal complete. She even went over board a few times. One year for Christmas she bought her boys a full-length pool table. However it was too big to fit in the living room and leave enough practical space for living and moving around for the living room. They played pool day in and day out until one day they came home and the pool table was gone. Doll had sold the table to a neighbor across the street. Doll was tired of running into the pool table and hurting herself. However, there were other things the boys had to play with, such as little green toy army soldiers with the trucks and tanks. Then there was the big red choo-choo train that they rode across the room on while pushing the horn. Not to mention the walkie- talkies she bought them. One year she bought them a drum and guitar set. They played with that drum and guitar until one afternoon when they were alone in the house. They decided to make some adjustments to the toys. When Doll returned to the house she found Darryl riding around on the guitar like it was a horse and Ronald was sitting inside the bass drum laughing. He had busted the bass of the drum and put water in it to make an in house personal swimming pool out of it. Needless to say they got a good whipping for destroying their toys and it was the last time they ever destroyed anything their mother gave them. Sometimes Doll would take her two sons down Nelson Street and look at Johnny Taylor, Little Milton and others sing songs before their stardom.

Indeed growing up in Greenville was full of good memories for Darryl and Ronald Baldridge. There were always people around who cared for them. Sheriff Davis was always around somewhere. Earline and Mary would stop in and see him. They were not rich, but they were not poor either. They had everything a child needed: love, safety, security, food, clothing, and shelter. Being a single-mother may not be the best way to raise a child. It certainly is not an easy task. However, with the support of trustworthy family a friends, a single parent can accomplish as much as any married parent. Earline "Doll" Baldridge proved this day in and day out.

Often times, Cousin Eric, or Demetria would keep the boys during the day. They played with them and taught them different things about growing up as young black males for Ronald. Back in those times, male role models were not in short supply like they are today. In fact, the very

25

term positive male role model was not even spoken like it is today. It was understood and expected that men would help out with children who did not have fathers. Men in the community were always mentoring nephews and nieces and neighborhood children in general.

Mary, or tee-tee as the boys called her, was another figure who was in the boys life growing up. Doll and her sister loved going fishing together down on the bank of the (Delta) Mississippi River. Darryl would brag on how many fish he caught while making fun of Ronald for not catching anything. On cool days the boys would tag along just to spend time with their tee-tee. Many times the boys would spend the night over at their tee-tees. Waking up over at her house in the morning would be full of good memories for them. She would ask her two nephews if she could fix any her two nephews of hers breakfast while they watched Popeye and other cartoons on television. Those words were their favorite words that their tee-tee said and she said them often. The boys would wake up to corn flakes with sugar, carnation milk, and toast with jelly. She kept it cold in the house, so they slept long and hard. The temperature felt good in the heat of the hot Mississippi summer.

One night, out of the blue, Ronald had an asthma attack. Doll put clothes on her two sons and they struck out to the hospital. Doll was scared but did not let her sons know it. All she would say is that Ronald needed help and God would protect them. There was not a lot of light on those roads back then, so it was difficult for them to see. The three of them was walking down a long dark road close to the side.

Suddenly, the headlights from a truck appeared. The truck had two white men in it. In those days, two white men in a pick up truck, late at night on a dark road meant trouble for a young black woman with children. The men passed Doll and her two sons and then came to a screeching stop. Doll saw the reverse lights of this truck light up and the truck began to back up towards them very quickly. The driver acted as if he were going to hit the three of them. Doll told them to get down as far off the road as possible and not to say anything, not even if the found her. Their little hearts were pounding a mile a minute as the truck turn around and rode back and forth, apparently in search of Doll and her two sons. Doll was scared to death. Not only were their two shady looking white men looking for them, but her baby was very sick and needed to get to the hospital fast. However, she remained calm for her children.

Finally, a policeman drove by in a car. She raised her head up and got the attention of the policeman. The officer helped her and her two sons in the car and drove them to the hospital. To this day, no one really knows what those two white men were wanted with Doll and her two boys.

Ronald would recover from the asthma attack, thank God. However, it was evident that Ronald would most likely continue to have sporadic and unpredictable asthma attacks if he did not receive proper medical treatment. The doctors in Greenville did not believe they were adequately equipped to treat a case as severe as Ronald's. So, they began to try to persuade Mrs. Baldridge to move to Memphis where the medical technology was more advanced and more suitable for cases such as Ronald's. Doll didn't want to move to Memphis because that was the place Dr. Martin L. King Jr. was killed at.

Doll found herself in a dilemma. She needed to make a decision and make it fast. Doll was very close to her sister Mary and the rest of the family in Greenville. Additionally, Darryl and Ronald loved their tee-tee. However, Ronald's health was very important. They had family in Memphis but they were closer to their family in Greenville. Doll knew deep down that she had to choose the well being of Ronald's long-term health.

The Big Move

Memphis, Tennessee

1972

While one sister was happy that Doll was moving to Memphis, the other one was not. Earline "Doll" Baldridge was not too happy herself about the move or leaving behind her sister. Even though they fought between each other, when push came to shove they were there for each in a heartbeat and Doll knew she could count on her sister Mary. She wasn't too sure she could depend on family in Memphis the way she depended on family in Greenville. However, Doll had to do what was necessary to insure the good health of her baby boy, Ronald. So, in 1972 Doll and her two boys moved to Memphis, Tennessee.

There first home was in some apartments on North Fifth Street in North Memphis. The down stairs apartment wasn't the best place to live, but Doll made it home like only a mother can. In the winter it would get so cold in the apartment that water would run down the busted pipe in the bathroom. Sometimes when the upstairs neighbor would run water, water would run down to the apartment below and flood the apartment bathroom where Doll and her boys lived.

Times were lean. Sometimes they didn't have enough meat in the pot for everyone. Doll would often times split what little meat there was between her two boys, while she ate corn bread and hot water gravy. Having to do without meat didn't bother Doll. She was glad that her to sons were full.

Girlie, Doll's oldest sister, was glad to have her baby sister in Memphis with her. Not knowing anyone in Memphis but her oldest sister, Doll would often bring her two boys over to see their Aunt. They loved their aunt very much, even though they didn't know her that well. Aunt Girlie was an excellent cook and had no difficulty winning the affection of her two nephews from Mississippi. Darryl and Ronald, or Renee as they called him, loved to eat her fried chicken, pinto beans with sugar, corn bread, and kool-aid. But most of all they loved her teacakes.

It was strange meeting their cousins for the very first time. They both wondered what they would say to them or how they would react to two new cousins coming from Greenville. They saw some young boys playing outside with a basket and a tire with dirt in it rolling it down the street, while another one was pushing a basket. "They're your cousins", their mother whispered to them as she pointed to the young boys playing outside. Darryl and Ronald approached the boys with some reservation. Darryl and Ronald introduced themselves to Toe, David, and Louis. Ronald and Toe formed an immediate bond, while Darryl gravitated toward David. You have to understand that both Ronald and Toe were full of spunk. They were both fighters. Darryl and David neither one would fight unless they had to. Later in the day, they met the rest of their cousins. The family started calling Ronald by his middle name, Renee. Darryl and Ronald grew up with a new friend whom their mother baby-sat sometimes; his name was Steve. Steve's mother had several children and he started to hang around Darryl and Ronald more and more, before long they were calling each other stepbrothers.

Sometimes Doll and her sister got into arguments about Doll's living situation. "Doll, you and those boys don't have to live in a apartment with water running down the pipes and flooding your place", Girlie would say to her sister in manner that seemed a lot like fussing. Girlie offered for her little sister to live with her for a while until she found a better place to live. Eventually, Doll found a place to live on Bickford Street in North Memphis. Doll didn't like to depend on anyone and the water was running into the apartment every so often.

Ronald was too young to go to school, so he would watch as his big brother went off to Caldwell Elementary School every day. Time seemed to stand still while Ronald waited for his big brother to get home from school. Ronald normal routine was Doll reading books to him, playing games, learning something from Electric Company on television, and helping his mother around the place. The most exciting part of the day for Ronald was seeing Darryl come up the street from school. Darryl would bring home his homework and Ronald would pretend to study with his brother. He called himself writing a sentence in cursive writing, imitating what he saw his brother doing. Ronald would write what he thought looked like a sentence in cursive and then show it to his mother. She always encouraged him to keep trying. After all, that is what a mother is supposed to do. She was trying teach her sons to think outside the box.

Doll had an uncle who helped them move to Memphis. This was the same uncle who used to fight off men who disrespected Doll when she was younger. His name was Uncle Isaac Simmons. He was bald, tall, slender, and had gotten older. He loved his niece and two great-nephews a great deal. There were many times that he would come and get his niece and great nephews and would take them out to dinner, to a movie or picnics. He would spend hours playing with the boys. Doll had three uncles: Isaac Simmons, Uncle Albert Simmons of Chicago, and Uncle Richard Simmons who lived in New York. However, Uncle Isaac was the closest to the family and the only uncle that the boys really ever met or knew at that time.

As the years went on, Uncle Isaac turned sick. At first he didn't want to tell his little niece and his great nephews. He felt she had a tough enough time adjusting to Memphis. She felt at times the family in Memphis wasn't very supportive of her. However, he eventually told the family that he was dying from cancer and there were nothing to be done. The doctors had given him all the medicine they could give him. Nothing was helping him recover. Soon after the announcement about Uncle Isaac's illness, the family received a phone call. They needed to get to the hospital fast. Twenty-four hours after the family was called into the hospital, Uncle Isaac Simmons was called home to glory. One of the only male influences in the boys' lives had left this earth. The family could not have known at that time how this loss would affect the boys, especially Ronald, in the future.

Spring arrived and Ronald once again found himself having difficulty breathing Earline gave him hot teas, Vick salves and hot coffees to drink to open his lungs. His stomach would ball up in knots like cramps and it caused him a great deal of pain, Doll would massage his stomach. Doll needed to get him to the doctor ASAP. She called from one house to the next in their Bickford Community. However, no one had time to take them.

31

Doll was once again reminded that people in Memphis not to be as supportive as people in Greenville were, and at the worst possible time. Doll and Ronald left out walking to what was then known as Toby Children's Hospital at John Gaston Hospital now The Regional Medical Center. Doll eventually was fortunate enough to run into one of her nephews who just happened to be driving down the street. However, what initially seemed like a fortunate coincidence quickly turned into a misfortune. She attempted to flag him down, but he kept going as if he didn't see them. It began to rain. Finally a friend of the family came by and took them to the hospital.

Visits to the hospital were always long and often times Ronald was admitted. Doll was always trying to be strong for her little baby boy, as they began to give him the routine I.V. drip. With tears in his eyes, Ronald tried to prepare himself for what he knew was about to take place. First came the alcohol wipe. Next came the warning before the stick of the needle. Finally, came the stick of the needle from the drip, followed by his scream and Doll's voice telling him to squeeze her hand.
Ronald would cry out with a loud voice "mommy please make it stop, make it go away". They would then tape his arm to a board to keep it straight. Doll always fought back the tears in her own eyes to be strong for her baby boy. She always told him to look at her when they began to stick him. Almost every time she called her big sister and Aunt Girlie would pick them up from the hospital listening to WLOK gospel radio station. They would laugh at their Aunt because she could smoke a cigarette and it move in her mouth and how the ash wouldn't move while she talked. There were times when Ronald would have to stay in the hospital because of asthma and the nurses would put plastic around the bed, which at times frightened him as a patient.

One summer evening, not long after the Baldridge family had moved to Memphis, the boys were outside playing football in front of what was called the Bickford Community Center. On this particular evening, a tall, brown skinned man walked out the community center and came over to the boys playing football in the front of it. He introduced himself as Melvin and asked all of them would they play sports for him. These sports would include football, basketball, and softball. They all said yes and the next day the gym opened up for those boys that were outside playing football the night before.

Inside the gym, the boys learned how to shoot basketball. Melvin taught them the fundamentals of basketball first. He showed them how to dribble with both hands, how to shoot free throws, lay ups, and defense. He got to know each and every child in that neighborhood by name. Sometimes the little boys would play basketball on the other end of the court and some bigger boys would try to take their goal or ball. Ronald and the rest of the little boys would go tell Melvin and he would make them get off the courts. Many times Melvin would let the boys on the major team play against the senior team to toughen them up. Melvin wasn't just a worker at Bickford he was Bickford best, trying to make a difference in the lives of hundreds of little boys and girls from all around North Memphis. He would continue to do so for many years to come. When there were good days you could find girls braiding guy's hair, others played with yo-yos, and others just hung out listening to music from G.Q., I destroyed your love by huff, or the O'Jays. Knocks on the different doors at times sharing sugar, flower, food and whatever else they could share in times of need .The neighborhoods were clean garbage was picked up and put into the garbage cans, grass was cut neatly, and flowers along with vegetables

were planted in yards by mothers and grandmothers. Ronald and Darryl didn't have any money to buy his mother a gift as a child so he made her something from Bickford at pottery classes. They made all types of pottery and Ronald made her a gift from the pottery class. Earline would smile and give them big hugs as they'd
stand there wishing her happy birthday.

Ronald's Elementary School Years

Memphis, Tennessee

1972-1979

 In August of 1972, the time finally came for Ronald to begin school. He was very excited about starting school and being just like his older brother Darryl. To Ronald, going to school was associated with being a big and Ronald believed that he was ready for the challenge of elementary academic rigor. However, his excitement was soon squashed. A few bad experiences at school did not help Ronald to form a positive opinion about school. One of the first experiences involved a conflict with another teacher. This not only made Ronald have an ill opinion about school, it also almost got his mother arrested. Oddly enough, this incident did not even take place in the Ronald's classroom.

Darryl, Ronald's older brother who was two years ahead of Ronald in school, had some profanity written on his book. The teacher saw these words and asked him who wrote it. Darryl was scared. He knew a boy they called Scalp, who was in Darryl's class, had written those words. However, he was afraid to get his friend in trouble, so he said his little brother wrote the words even though he knew Ronald did not write those words. Ronald did not even know how to write such words at that age.

The teacher asked Ronald to come to her class and she asked him to pronounce the word. Of course Ronald could not pronounce the word; he could not even read the word. That's when the teacher made a big mistake. She hit him in the back then sent him back to his class. Later that evening, Ronald told his mom what happened. Doll was furious. She was so upset that her sister had to calm her down before she went to the school. Doll wanted to beat that woman with in an inch of her life for touching her son. She took him to Toby children hospital.

The next day came and Doll escorted her two sons to school. Doll confronted the teacher and was able to control her temper. The teacher apologized to Mrs. Baldridge and also to Ronald. Doll accepted her apology and the matter was resolved without any verbal or physical violence. However, Doll made it crystal clear to the principal and teacher that they were to call her if any conflicts arose in the future. Under no circumstances was anyone at the school to hit her sons without consent from her.

Ronald did not have any more altercations with that particular teacher, but he still did not like School. The school was too crowded. Some mornings, the students would have to wait for someone to open the back door to let them inside the school. He wanted his mother to take him out of that school.

Ronald eventually got his wish and was able to transfer from Caldwell Elementary to Grant Elementary. Ronald loved that school. He had a good teacher named Mrs. Sanders. Each morning before school began Ronald would meet up with a new friend everyone called Truck. They would play together and over the next several years, they developed a close friendship. Ronald wasn't a perfect child and did wrong, even at the new school. However, Earline refused to give up on her two sons even if it meant disciplining them. That's what happens if you are a young mother and you have children at an early age. Some young mothers think when you have sons you can't discipline them because they are to big and tall. Earline did not believe that. Earline would continue to discipline until she died, a positive male role model came into their lives, or they got the picture. She would sit her two sons down and talk to them about life and how to talk to people. She taught them how to shake another man's hand while looking them in their eyes, clean house, how to dress, and how to carry themselves. Earline taught her sons keep their shirt in their pants. Smacky was a short chubby boy from the neighborhood who was older than Ronald and Darryl. He was basketball player at Manassas High School. Darryl and Ronald would often run into Smacky at the gym at Bickford Community Center. Everyone at Bickford received a nickname from Smacky. In1979, while Ronald was still at Grant, Ronald got the name Lizard. He was called Lizard because he had tight eyes. Toby children hospital closed down and another children hospital opened, Le Bonheur Children hospital. That's where Earline would take Ronald to or, as Dr. Duncan would say "little Ronald". His allergy doctor at Le Bonheur hospital was Dr. Duncan. Ronald was crazy about his female doctor that was a Native American with very long hair. Ronald enjoyed going Le Bonheur because the nurses gave him sprites drinks, candy, ice cream and if he was in the hospital for a holiday they got gifts. Ronald thought to himself what a wonderful hospital.

The 70's were good times and the memories would last for years to come. Summer days were filled with the games children played back then. On many evenings, before it got dark, all the kids in the neighborhood would get together and play football in the parking lot of what would soon become the Bickford Community Center. The children would also get together and play games like hide and seek, catch a girl kiss a girl, red rover, and tag.

There were many days all the children would meet up at Bickford Park to play hockey sticks, volleyball, outside basketball, and horseshoes and wait on the lunch truck in the summer. Sometimes they would have milk fights with each other and laugh about it later. Their mothers would sometimes get on them about messing up their clothes. Summer also provided opportunities to spend the night with relatives. This was something that only happened on weekends and during emergency situations during the school year. One day during the summer Earline and Girlie took the family out to Millington to see Al Green home and to visit their cousins. This day Ronald, Darryl, David, Toe and some others went to the back to look at the animals. Some of their cousins tried to push them over into the fence that had a wild pig. Of course they started screaming and family came running to get them out the fence and Girlie gave her son a whipping.

That same night Ronald and Darryl spent the night with their cousin, Toe. Ronald and Toe saw this raccoon out in the back yard. Being mischievous little boys, Ronald decided that he wanted to catch it. Suddenly, Toe heard someone shouting out loud. It was Ronald. The raccoon had attacked Ronald and tore his pants up. Ronald came around the house running for his life and scared to death. Toe just fell out laughing at his cousin.

It was a good year and around the time a new, young, eager black man Harold Ford Sr. who was running for United States Congress. This was good for the black-community in Memphis, and particularly good for those in North Memphis. This young man was asking for financial, voting and volunteer support from the Bickford Community Center residents, as well as reassuring the members of the community that he would be able to help them once he is elected into office. Doll attended each of those meetings with Darryl and Ronald each on a knee as they looked on. She didn't know at that time that she would eventually end up campaigning for him for the next year and for a long time afterward. In fact, Doll got to know the family of this man who was running for Congress very well and eventually worked for one of his family members who was a doctor.

On June 10 1978, Doll and the boys took a trip back to Greenville to visit their Aunt and cousins. They visited old friends and family. Earline, or Doll as she was known in Greenville, went to see old friends on Nelson Street like the Sheriff of the city and the women who fixed her hair during the time of Dr. King's death in Memphis. They had missed their family back home, but after a four-day visit, the time came to return to Memphis. The trip was fun and fulfilling in multiple ways. However, what the family came home to was not quite so pleasant. While they were gone. Some thieves had broken into their apartment. The robbers had stolen Doll's fur coat, fur stove, fur hats, and all their personal belongings. The family was crushed. Doll was particularly crushed. After all, she had worked hard to buy those items. Someone in the neighborhood knew who was responsible for this act, but no one was saying anything.

Sometimes the boys would get into fights with other boys. These other boys would often get their bigger brothers or cousins to help them fight Toe, David, Darryl, Ronald and the rest of their cousins. Darryl and

Ronald also sometimes called on their cousins for assistance in these fights, when things got out of hand. It looked as if they were getting into fights at least once a week. After all, Girlie had twelve children. Pole Bean was the cousin most called upon by Darryl and Ronald during these times of distress with older, bigger children. Pole Bean would usually just watch these neighborhood fights. When he saw bigger children or adults get involved in it then, and only then, is where he would come into the fight with his brothers and other nephews. Walking across the park with confidence and poise, Pole Bean told the bigger kids to not touch Darryl and Ronald. He would follow this command with an ultimatum; leave his nephews alone or suffer the consequences from him and his family. Earline would whip her two sons often trying to teach them the right way of respect and to stay out of trouble.

When Ronald was ten and Darryl was twelve, Doll began dating. Certain men would take Doll out to dinner and sometimes a movie. Afterwards, Doll would sometimes invite these men into the house, but only for a brief visit. She never allowed them to stay very long. After all, she had two young boys and she was not going to disrespect them like that. On one particular night, the man Doll had gone out with began to pressure Doll into letting him spend the night. When she flat out said no, he began arguing with her. He felt that because he spent money on her, he should move in for the night. Doll protested that as she walked into the kitchen. He crept up behind her and knocked her down. Doll didn't even know what hit her. Ronald and Darryl heard their mom shout and they ran into the kitchen just in time to see him trying to hit her again. Doll kicked him up off of her and Ronald grabbed a very sharp hook blade off the table and jumped up and cut him at the top of his back pulling the hook blade down his back. The guy grabbed his back screaming while blood was shooting out everywhere as he ran out the apartment back door. Darryl grabbed a skillet and hit him with it. Darryl ran to their Aunt's house up the street to let them know what took place. Ronald would never forget that night.

You should have seen the family coming to her aid. Ronald was very proud to have older cousins who had their back. That day the two brothers vowed no man would ever touch their mother again without paying a heavy price; and the price would be death. The two boys kept that vow.

Now Ronald was taught to respect adults as a child and he never went looking for fights. However, when trouble found him, he was the type of child who believed in handling his business. Trouble certainly did find Ronald from time to time, and on one particular occasion trouble came in the form of a little boy who liked to start trouble by lying on people. This little boy lied about Ronald stealing something. Ronald warned the boy to stop telling lies. However, the little boy ignored Ronald's warning and continued to falsely accuse Ronald. Ronald handled his business. However, this incident was far from settled. Earline would sit her two sons down and talk to them about cooking, cleaning, going to school getting a job and reason for staying out of trouble. This day would be no different she sat them down after they had finished dinner to talk about drugs, alcohol and the reason not to do them. Earline, Ms. Lillian, and Dolly were neighbors and they would hang out in front of the apartments talking while looking over toward Bickford Community Center. These were just some of the neighbors back then when Ronald would get caught doing something wrong. Earline had given them permission to tear the butts up and there were many days Ronald would get a whipped by the neighbor then by his mother. It was those types of people, neighbors and friends that made the difference. They stuck together in more ways than one. That kept crime down and taught children to be respectful toward the elderly.

One day Ronald was walking to the park to play basketball with his friends, brother, and cousins. The mother of the child came around the corner and called herself going to give Ronald the beating of a lifetime. She was sadly mistaken. She swung at Ronald and missed. Ronald asked her to leave him alone while blocking her swings. Finally he had enough and decided that the best defense in this situation was a good offense. He delivered two punches to the face and a couple of times in the stomach. He picked her picked her up and body slammed her on the ground. Then, Ronald pulled her son's shirt over his head then sprung on the little boy and kicked him. Darryl saw what was going on and ran over to stop it but it was too late. Darryl called for his cousin Toe who was playing basketball on the outside court. Ronald had beat the woman up and left her there crying. This was the first of many fights that Ronald would finish.

One night, a year later, Darryl and Ronald were at the house when suddenly the sound of sirens rang out in the night air. A knock came on the door. It was one of their neighbors coming to tell them that a man who tried to talk to her hit their mom in the head with a pipe. He got angry with her because she blew him off. Darryl and Ronald stood there scared, angry, and worried about their mother. Their aunt tried to comfort them, but all they thought about was their mom. Earline came home from the hospital and went on with her life. From that point on she had headaches and both boys vowed when they were older they were going to make sure he paid severely.

They started to follow him and made sure they remembered his face very well so they could repay him. Doll recovered from her injury. Many months later Ronald saw the guy that hit his mom in the head. He followed the guy without his knowledge until he stopped. It was time for Ronald to repay him for the pain he caused his mom. The man walked into the store on Chelsea Avenue, but as he was coming out of the store he got into it with another man. Ronald watched the guy he was going to hurt get into a fight with another man in front of the store. Ronald witnessed the man that hit his mom in the head get back what he had done to Doll. That night, the man that had caused Doll to suffer from headaches to this day got hit in the head with a jack iron by another man and was out cold with blood running out of his head. The man just laid there shaking. Ronald wanted to walk up on him and beat him some more, but instead he just watched and wondered if the man was going to die. Ronald went away feeling relieved that something had happened to the guy that hurt his mother. He felt no sorrow for him at all.

From that point, Ronald began to grow cold and callus. Now there wasn't much trouble going on in their family that normally would include whole family involvement. One evening, a knock came on the door of Earline .It was one of her nephews. He said grandmother said come quickly. One of Earline's nieces had gotten into a fight with another woman and her family. Earline grabbed her handgun and ran down to her sister's house. Ronald, Darryl and his cousins Toe, David, Louis, Fat and others were all watching from a good hide out spot. That's when it happened. A car was coming down the street. It was the woman and her family. They had come to give Earline's niece a beaten of her life. That's what they thought, because gunfire started coming from behind trees and cars. Gunfire came from inside the house of her niece and other places. Earline, her older sister, nephews, nieces and other family would be right by her sister's side shooting guns at the woman and her family. Ronald, Darryl and his cousins watched as they saw their entire family get into a shootout with another family. It was a blessing that no one got shot or killed. The family feud would end and life would get back to normal, as they knew it.

You see Ronald, just like his mother, was a survivalist even at a young age. Ronald found a way to try to make sure anyone who tried to come at him once, didn't come at him again. The more time passed, the more Ronald saw, the more deviant Ronald became. He wouldn't start fights, but he would make sure he finished them. Ronald and his cousin Toe, who was also his best friend and constant companion, believed in the concept better to be judged by twelve than carried by six. This belief would further direct their actions for many years to come. Those two would get into a fight with someone every other day it seemed.

The children in the neighborhood all got along sometimes as if they were family. Summer times were the best you had to prove yourself in the neighborhood between the boys to see if they would fight back, if they fought back they were accepted in the neighborhood and the fellows. This is what happened to a young light skinned boy named Michael. Michael and the rest of the boys became good friends. He came up to Bickford Community Center to play ball. One of the guys from the neighborhood was guarding Michael in basketball game but couldn't keep him from scoring and tried to fight him. Michael started hitting the guy all over. They broke it up while accepting Michael into the fellows and the neighborhood. Ronald was short but he didn't take anything off of any one no matter how big they were. One summer afternoon David their cousin and He Haw a friend of Darryl and Ronald were walking in Bickford Park. They noticed Ronald telling another boy much older than him to leave him alone. They noticed Ronald had with him a baseball bat in his hand. Suddenly, a loud crack rang out in the air. His cousins and a friend looked over where they had just seen Ronald and the big boy arguing. Now there was only Ronald standing there. The other kid was on the ground. Ronald had hit the boy as hard as possible with the bat several times. Luckily the boy did not die, but he did suffer several broken bones, bloody nose. No one ever said a word about Ronald hitting that boy. You just didn't snitch in the hood because everyone helped everyone.

Middle School Years
Memphis, Tennessee
1979-1980

1980 was the year Ronald and Darryl went to Humes Junior High School. That school was off the chain. Students played ball in the gym every morning, it was always packed with kids. Darryl, Scalp, Steve, Wee-Wee, Lakeith, Knotty, Devil, Ronald and the other guys was always shooting hoops in the gym early every morning, drinking before class and girls were everywhere looking fine. The kids were creative in their style of dressing back then. Some people wore jeans with their names wrote on them with markers and spray painted. Others wore Izod shirts with khakis and one sock matching the color of pants and the other matched the shirt. Baggy pants was out back then and, the fellows in the hood wore suit coats in the summer and trench coats in the winter because they carried sawed offs shot guns. Humes was one of those schools that you wanted to go to because they had after school dances and it was always packed with girls from everywhere.

Middle school proved to be more popular with Ronald than elementary school. One reason was that there were more opportunities for social interaction and less structure. They danced to the music of The Times, Morris Day, Barkays, the Gap Band and others. Those songs would have an impact on Ronald that he would not be aware of at the time he entered 7th grade simply put, it was good music. Since school was starting Earline thought she'd have the talk with her two sons about sex. She called them into the living room and asked them to sit down she needed to talk to them. She started to talk to them and asked them have they had sex yet, they both lied and said no. She told them something that Ronald would remember and try to live by for the rest of his life. She told them if you ever find a woman that will love you and can laugh with you through the worst times. So when the good times come they are great times. Someone who is willing to plant a seed of a tree, watch it, nurture it and when the tree grows the two of you can live under the shade of the tree. That woman you marry. Earline was the mother and father like most of the women were. In those times

Every year, at the end of a basketball season, Melvin would give the boys and girls a banquet to show his appreciation to them for playing for him. They had a variety of food, music, and afterward a dance. Some of the kids had an eating contest going on between them and Ronald won it by eating 20 pieces of fried chicken by himself. Melvin would sometimes get the okay from Mr. Henderson, who was the director at that time, to set up the gym as a skating rink. The kids skated from 7:00 p.m. until 9:00 p.m.

Earline and her two sons had this hobby. They would get together on the weekends and watch Soul Train, Roller Derby, and Kung fu at night while eating rice. They'd laugh and joke as their mom sometimes talked about how things were when she was a child; Darryl and Ronald loved listening to her talk about her life. It's unfortunate that children today don't do those things anymore. Ronald was fascinated with how they survived, the things people went through, and the determination to survive through the struggle.

Toe and Ronald was walking down Seventh Street at night when these two pretty woman in their late 20's called them up to their house. They were hesitant to go up but both were strapped with guns. They went to the outside of the house talking to the women when the women asked them to come in. They went inside and there it was. There was beer, wine, and whiskey on the table by the gallon. Ronald and Toe were not adults but they were big for their age. The women poured them a couple of drinks. They drank them after they saw the women drinking the alcohol. Before long they were drunk and they started to dance with the women. All of a sudden they were standing in front of the couch and the women pushed them back onto the couch and had their way with the two boys. They never told their mothers about it because they couldn't believe they had two women.

It was around this time that a white van was going around Memphis trying to kidnap children. The van contained two white males and they targeted black children in predominately black neighborhoods. One particular night Steve, who was a very close friend with Ronald, was on his way home when a van fitting the description of the van everyone had been warned about approached him. Two white males made a swift attempt at trying to snatch him dressed as women. Steve ran as fast as he could up into Bickford and told Melvin what had occurred.

Melvin went into protect mode and grabbed his famous baseball bat that he used as an equalizer. The kids at Bickford Center had watched Melvin swing that bat on many occasion to stop trouble before it got out of hand. Melvin took off after that van and everyone else followed, but unfortunately was unable to find it. At that time, Melvin had this long blue Cadillac. The car was so big he could fit eight children in the car. He used his car to transport the basketball team when they played against the kids at Sexton. Melvin wasn't just a coach to hundreds of boys that played for Bickford. He was also a mentor, father figure, friend, uncle, big brother, and protector. No memorial, monument, or tribute could ever express what Melvin meant to the kids in the Bickford neighborhood. Snow covered the city that day. Michael and Rob cut class same day and Toe and Ronald got them to go down town while it had just snowed. They went buying clothes, eating food from money that they had recently come into and end up helping people push their cars out the snow. Bickford had yo-yo, shuffleboard, pool, ping-pong and card contests. On Halloween the rest rooms in the gym would become haunted house .The older kids from the neighborhood were the ghost, monsters and other creatures. The rest of the parents in return would patrol the streets with the younger kids so none would snatch their bags of treats. Time had passed Steve and others were in the library at Bickford in the hallway. Steve walked over to one of the open doors in the hallway and one of the staff at Bickford slammed Steve's finger up in the door accidentally. He and Ronald screamed as they beat on the door to get them to open it, his finger was smashed up and twisted with blood shooting out everywhere. Melvin rushed him to the hospital as he watched Steve in pain and agony. The finger healed and Steve got better, he went back to playing basketball.

While the boys were at school, Doll and a lady named Mrs. Swift was away from home working at the thrift store. Mrs. Swift was an elderly woman who loved the Lord as well as children. One day the boys came to the thrift store and Mrs. Swift asked the boys would they be interested in going to church with her. They said yes and from that point on she would come and pick them up for Church from time to time.

Doll made other new friends, as well. Mrs. Shaw was a very good friend of hers. Those two would hustle for everything when it came to food or making money. They slaughtered hogs, cut them up, and divided it between themselves, along with chickens, peas, corn, and any other kind of food that could be raised in the back yard or in a garden. Over the years, Mrs. Shaw and Doll would develop a close relationship. Red Earline was another person who had a close relationship with Doll. The women in this close group of friend called her Red Earline, since Doll's name was also Earline. However, Doll's leisure time did not always involve friends. Sometimes Doll and her nephew Pole Bean would go to his brothers night club off North Seventh Street, where they would step to the music of Johnnie Taylor's *If I Could Turn Back the Hands of Time*. Doll would say to Pole Bean, "come on nephew, let's show them how to dance", and those two would dance until the early hours of the next morning. Toe and Ronald wanted to get away for a while and started walking together over to one of their cousins house and out of no where one of Ronald's older cousins said to their faces that they won't make it to the age 18 and they were the black sheep of the family. They both looked at each other with disbelief that a family member would say something like that to them. It both hurt them and made them angry, as they walked up the streets they looked at 201 Poplar and said they was never going to go to jail ever.

In 1980, Ronald was 13 years old. You didn't attack or involve people families into the problem. The code was respected by many every once in a while someone would violate. When that happened Niggas got drugged out their shoes for violating family rules. After receiving the news that Ronald's brother, Darryl had been jumped by some of the boys from North Seventh Street, Ronald and his cousin Toe went to retrieve their gun from their cousin, Pole Bean. They wanted theirs just in case they had to use it. Pole bean didn't want to give the gun back to them. He thought he was going to take the gun from them and even attempted to fire a shot at Ronald and Toe, his own flesh and blood. The two boys grabbed Pole Bean from behind and took their gun so that they could handle their business. It didn't matter at that time to Toe and Ronald that Pole Bean was their cousin. Someone had jumped on Darryl for no reason at Bickford Community Center. Darryl had nothing to do with the previous fights and the boys from North Seventh Street were wrong for jumping him.

Toe and Ronald went to Bickford a couple of days later hoping to see one of the boys that had jumped Darryl there. Art, one of the brothers of the boys from North Seventh Street, was up at Bickford playing basketball. Toe ran up on him and hit him before he knew it. Ronald swung at the brother but missed. The brother who had been innocently hoping just minutes ago now found himself trapped between Ronald and Toe. Ronald had the gun in a paper sack. Truck a close friend was close by looking at the fight when Ronald pulled out the gun, accidentally dropping it on the floor. It didn't go off. Ronald picked up the gun while Toe and Art, the brother from North Seventh Street, were fighting. Art ran toward the gym door to get out and Ronald started shooting at his head, missing it by inches while running behind him. Art ran track in school and his running skills were extremely useful that day. He was running for his life because Ronald was a step behind him and inches from filling his head with lead. Later on Art and his brothers came to them and asked for forgiveness, but that did not matter a lot to Ronald and Toe. They didn't mind hurting or dying for family and true close friends. You don't find to many dogs willing to bark in the dark. In spite of what went on in their neighborhood. The boys who were growing up in the neighborhood became increasingly concerned about threatening activities, such as purse snatching, robberies, and home break-ins in general. Knowing that police protection was not thorough enough to provide the protection they felt that their mothers deserved, they began patrolling the neighborhoods themselves. These boys had eaten at each other's houses, slept in each other's beds, and basically lived as if they were family rather than friends.

They decided to make a pact that no one would come into their community and hurt their mothers, the elderly, or the children that lived there. Both sides of Chelsea came together and fought other guys that came into their neighborhood to steal, rob, break into homes, or abuse a girl from their hood. North Memphis was straight and consisted of a variety of neighborhoods other than Bickford. Each of these neighborhoods had their own group of young men who represented and protected. Smokey City had the notorious the Family and Hurt Village had their own crew, which consisted of Tatter, Daryl, Head, Donald, and the twins. There was also New Chicago, located near Manassas High School. Without a doubt North Memphis had their own different crews throughout the area. They called themselves the *Night Hawks*. The name *Night Hawks* was taken from a motorcycle group out of Chicago. The *Night Hawks* went to Humes Junior High, Manassas High School, Northside High School, Memphis Tech, and Westside High School.

One day in 1982 at Bickford Robert, one of the *Night Hawks*, came to the park with a couple of white teens to play football. They were told of an abandoned white building on North Second Street. Erby, Darryl, Michael, and the rest of the guys from Bickford came up with an idea to turn that house into a haunted house. The boys from the hood, as they often called themselves, worked hard to make this house scary. After all of the hard work, the house had a scene from the *Texas Chainsaw Massacre*, cow bones, fake blood, Frankenstein, and a host of other monsters. Ronald dressed up like a vampire and hid behind the second entrance door.

They knew there was an outdoor entrance into a basement, but they had no idea at the time what the purpose of that basement had been. They later found out it was an <u>Underground Railroad hide out for runaway slaves</u>. The money they made with the haunted house was used to help the elderly who didn't have enough money for rent or lights. The Night Hawks also would pitch in and have dances at Bickford Community Center, car washes, or cook outs and give the money to the elderly to help them to pay their bills. True that the boys from the hood had a good time, but they felt good about taking back their neighborhood and establishing some control over what went on in their streets. There were rules to the streets, even in gangs. They didn't kill each other even though they had guns. It was about community they would stick together.

However, none were hated as much as the B Family often referred to as simply *The Family*. The Nighthawks and the Family fought on a consistent basis. One time after school one of the Nighthawks went over to a girl's house in Smokey City and was caught by The Family and was beaten severely. Another time, Nod, a friend of the Family who happened to live in the Bickford community, was at the Bickford Community Center. All the boys in Bickford gym was playing basketball. Nod was playing basketball and he was harassing and talking bad to the opponent he was guarding. He kept fouling him on the hand. Finally the opponent of Nod asked him to stop. Eric, Ronald and the rest of the guys in the gym watched as Nod tried to dump the opponent on the floor. The boy hit Nod on the side of the face by his hairline and was knock him out cold while Melvin ran in with a couple of wet paper towels to wake Nod. Donny another guy who was playing basketball was counting him out down on the other end of the court in the gym. Eric and the rest of the people in the gym couldn't help from laughing at Nod for trying to be tough. It took him a while to realize where he was.

The Nighthawks would fight the Family on various occasions. One such fight took place at Humes due to retaliation from a previous fight that was lost. Darryl and Ronald had just left Humes when some of the Nighthawks from Westside High School came over to tell Darryl and Ronald that there was going to be a the fight with the Family against some of the guys from Lauderdale Court. Darryl and Ronald decided not to stick around, so they headed to the house. Meanwhile, the Family jumped the other Nighthawks. A few days later, the Family jumped a friend of the Nighthawks. This meant war. Some of the Nighthawks, including Ronald, went to Humes to confront the Family. One of the members of the Family ran out of the gym at Humes in order to jump one of the Nighthawks. Suddenly, shots rang out. He had been shot by one of the members of the Nighthawks. After the shooting, the Nighthawks jumped him and beat him mildly. The Nighthawks then dispersed rapidly. These types of retaliations were common among gangs in Memphis back then. Unfinished business did not stay unfinished for long. The B Family would retaliate against the Night Hawks and vice versa. The Gangster Disciples would fight the Vice Lords and the Vice Lords would retaliate against The Gangster Disciples.

One day toward the end of Ronald's junior high school career, the Night Hawks got into another big fight with some guys off North Seventh Street in Bickford gym over a basketball game in the pool room. Rome, who was an enemy of the Night Hawks from North Seventh Street, was one of the individuals involved in the scuffle. He went to school at Humes and decided he was going to hide out up at the school. He didn't know that Ronald, Darryl, Cocaine, and the other Night Hawks went up to the school looking for him. They caught him coming out of the school and Cocaine hit Rome in the face from one side while knocking him toward Ronald and Toe. They both pulled nun-chucks out at the same time and hit him with nun-chucks from each side. They broke his jaw and he had to use wires in his mouth for months following the fight. However, this would not be the end of this fight.

Right before Ronald was to start high school, trouble from the previous fight reared its ugly head and the Night Hawks once again found themselves in defense mode. Many of the Night Hawks believed that the best defense was a good offense. Carrying this belief deep in their soul with conviction, they found it necessary to have weapons. They normally did not carry the weapons on them, but rather had the weapons hidden in a place that was easily accessible to them when it became necessary to defend with force. In fact, earlier that month Ronald, Toe, and all the other Night Hawks had cut off the iron legs of chairs and made nun-chucks out of them and they taught each other how to use them. They became very skilled in the use of the nun-chunks and other weapons like guns, knives, cocktails, and brass knuckles. They invented methods ways to hurt people and defend themselves.

High School
Memphis, Tennessee
1981-1985

When it was time for Ronald to enter high school, Ronald had no problem making the decision to leave Humes Jr. High School and enroll into Westside High. Most of his friends and family were at Westside High School in the Frayser area. Westside was small, but the Nighthawks ran the school. This was an important advantage because there are always going to be times when young men had to fight other young men in high school. However, for the most part, the young boys from Bickford had a good time. They would pull foolish pranks; such as the time they stole all of the breakfast the morning their bus beat everyone to the school. The Night Hawks went into the cafeteria and saw no one there. So they took the crates of juices, milk, and food to their hide out in the back of the shed on school campus to eat it, and then left the evidence behind. This prank cost the entire school the privilege of eating breakfast at school for three months. They also were notorious for hustling for a few dollars to purchase some Wild Irish Rose Wine to drink before the school bus arrived to pick them up and carry them to school. They'd all walk down the hallway together and force the other students to move out of the way. One day at school they convinced some of the guys playing kick ball to pull their shorts down and kick the ball to the girls. One of the boys pulled his shorts and underwear all the way down to his knees and was kicked out of school.

Several days later, Toe and Ronald decided to cut class at lunch time. Unfortunately, Toe wore red that day. They were hiding in the back of the school drinking when the principal saw the red Toe had on and caught them. They went to the office and got licks for trying to cut class and a phone call to their parents. No Earline didn't know that Ronald cut class but when he got home that day he got a serious beating after she discussed why she disciplined him. Earline had this favorite saying and it was "I brought you in this world and I'll take you out". Ronald and Darryl didn't want to cause problems for their mother. They realized the three of them were all each other had. Ronald watched his mother visit his school to see how he was doing. She made sure they had their schoolwork. Earline came in from work and cooked dinner, being super mother.

One afternoon, Ronald was pulled into the kitchen by a smell that was making him hungry, and Earline was not even home yet. It was his brother Darryl cooking dinner for his mother and he was trying to surprise her. When she came through the doors and smelled food she thought she left something cooking, until Darryl told her they were cooking for her and she grabbed both of them and kissed and hugged them. From that point forward, Darryl and Ronald did the cooking. They wanted to help their mother in any way they could. They knew they had to work together in order to survive in the world. Family is important no matter what. Mothers need to continue to encourage, discipline and motivate their children to be the best in life they can be. Ronald was a hard head teen that needed a foot on his neck sometimes by a man. What does a single mother do when she is doing all she can to raise two young boys by herself? She finds a positive male role model for them to talk to, hang out with, go to movies and etc.

One particular year Christmas came and it was cold outside. Michael called Toe and called Ronald, Soon the word got around to meet up in Bickford Park so they could all play football together. They enjoyed that like never before. Who'd ever think to play football on Christmas but that was just the way they were. They enjoyed their youth and doing active sports kept them from being over weight, one reason was they didn't have a lot of video games. They got skate boards, basketballs, drums, and scooters. The fun came when it would snow and they would play football games in it.

They continued to play basketball at Bickford Community Center. Each Community Center had basketball teams and they would visit each other's Community Centers and play each other. Each gym had Pee-Wee, juniors, seniors, and Majors. Just about every boy in the neighborhood played in all four-age brackets. Melvin was that male role model for them. He was a lot of things to the teenagers in the area. Melvin would talk to all of them about how to handle problems. Sometimes that meant giving the boys gloves and a mat and letting them fight it out. Melvin would let them play whole court basketball games. Those were good times. They played against each other for a case of beer. Darryl would come down pull up and hit with a jump shot. Ronald would give the ball to Bob and they would go down, drive to the goal, and pass it off to Steve. It was money in the bank. Others would be waiting their down to play ball, while some played spades. It was a fun time; they had dances, played horseshoes and football. Michael, Pete, Toe and the others would be in the back room of Bickford working on dance moves because they were interring a dance contest on Mid America Mall.

When the weather turned hot, fights were practically a daily occurrence. Now the Nighthawks had a rival gang that they fought on a regular basis. Other neighborhoods feared this gang of guys because there were so many of them and they didn't care about hurting you. The Vice Lords was around and caused problems but not like this other gang. However, this gang, known as simply The Family, met their match when it came to the Nighthawks, for Toe, Ronald and a few others didn't care about hurting others either. The Family had a leader everyone called Bone he had some notorious members. The boys from Bickford would find themselves in numerous altercations with this crew. The Night Hawks had respect for everyone from each area because that was the way of North Memphis. The word had spread around Bickford that a new director was coming over to Bickford over Melvin. They hoped he would be like Melvin. The day came and the director came over while they were shooting a game of basketball.

From nowhere the director started disrespecting some of the fellows. First he put Duboy out the gym, then he told Ronald, Toe, Fred, Darryl, Michael, Boone and some others to get out for a week. They all meet up at the table in the park and discussed what they were going to do. They all walked around to the parking lot and looked at his car. They kept walking toward the car. They all got on one side of the car and turned his car over. The new director came outside to go home because he was off from work. He could not believe what he saw, his car turn over. The next day he came to work he tried to find out who had done that. No one would communicate with him about the car. He learned to respect all the people over there in the neighborhood.

One afternoon at Westside High School, the Nighthawks got a call that Darryl was in trouble with the Family over at Northside High School, where he attended. Darryl did not go to Westside with Ronald and the rest of the Nighthawks. Even though it was the middle of the day, the Nighthawks from Westside walked from Westside to Northside High School with sawed off 12 gauges in their jackets. Once they reached the school, they entered through the back way and went up the steps. A crowd of teens was at their lockers. Some members of the Imperial Gents, a quasi-social fraternity at Northside, came upstairs. The Nighthawks asked one of the Imperial Gents where Darryl was. The Imperial Gents informed them that Darryl had walked home with their girl cousin, Pee-wee. Darryl was laid back and didn't like to fight unless force to boxing had taught him that. Someone mentioned that the Principal was coming and Toe and Ronald took out running, getting away from the school. They went looking for Darryl at Bickford Community Center, but he was not there. They later learned that he had went to Pee-Wee' s house. This was an incident that could have ended much worse than it did. Lives could have been taken and young boys could have been injured. It was fortunate that none of this transpired. However, things would not always go as smoothly, especially considering that Ronald was about to become deeper involved in gang activities.

Every morning the gang would all met up at the bus stop to talk. The liquor store was always in their view. Some mornings before they went to school they'd stop there and get their favorite drink, Wild Irish Rose. More mornings that not, the gang would be drunk by the time the bus driver arrived. Some times their bus driver would race with other buses to the school.

Becoming A Gangster Disciple

1982 was the year Ronald was introduced to G, who was a member of the Gangster Disciples. Now G was "a real go get him" He had a crew of enforcers that was seldom seen until needed. He asked Ronald if he would be interested in becoming a member. Ronald said yes and Ronald was blessed into the Nation as an enforcer by doing some dirt. An enforcer is someone that keeps other gang members in line, usually by using physical violence against the out of line members. Made sure others respected their parents, attempted to make good grades in school and respected their parents. G had given Ronald a list of codes, signs, and their meanings. Laws and policies to learn what signs to throw to others. They wanted to make sure everything was kept a secret. They just didn't say BOSS to anyone or let anyone in without checking them out first, besides a coward was not welcome. For the next few years, Ronald would deliver what is known as the pumpkin head, which involves kicking and/or hitting someone in the head repeatedly until their head swells like a pumpkin with bats. The two of them would travel up and down the road together. Vice lords love to start trouble for one reason or another. From a far they would hear the word" five popping six dropping, their reply six to the sky 5 gotta die". Many times it was just talk as they laughed at each while walking passed a Vice Lord. You see they could be in the same area without trying to kill each other. Especially when trouble was thick they'd call G and his Folks. Sometimes they would play others from different neighborhoods in football, they like having fun as well. This particular evening both the Night hawks and , the Gangster Disciple got together to play football. They all lined up for the snap , Toe ran deep Michael threw him the ball. Toe had his eyes on the ball getting ready to catch it all of a sudden an old man named Mr. Fish was walking across the grass. Mr. Fish hit Toe in the head with a brick for no reason and ran. Everyone ran to Toe's aide. The old man was gone; they stopped playing ball and helped Toe. They took him to the hospital while others were looking for the old man. Before they could catch up with him, Toe's brother found him and beat him badly.

Ronald and the other boys in the neighborhood hung out doing all kind of things, some bad some good. One favorite thing the fellows would get together and have cookouts, play bones, and listen to music. They would see preachers walking past them coming out of the stores, parks, and other places but still they didn't show any concern about not just their soul but them. Many pastors were afraid of them, when Jesus wouldn't have. They didn't know why. Some preachers and pastors would jump in the car and speeding off afraid they were going to ask them for something. They were just trying to find their way in a world so big at that time. It was a hot day in Spring Toe and Ronald hung together like Nod and Wee-Wee, they were playing basketball outside. Toe and Wee-Wee went to the store to get some drinks. They were laughing and tripping about girls and other things that was funny to them on the way back to the park. Mean while back on the court Nod and Ronald gets into it over the game. Ronald was smacked by Nod and Ronald grabbed him kneed him in the stomach. Just then Toe and Wee-Wee came around the corner, they saw what was going on and they dropped their drinks and started fighting against each other. Ronald had Nod on the ground. Wee-Wee tackled Ronald and started trying to choke him. Toe grabbed Nod and was punching and kicking him. Melvin ran out and broke up the fight.
The Family continued to attack Night Hawks and vice versa. One evening, Humes Junior High was having a basketball game. Some of the guys wanted to go over to the game. Toe, Ronald, Darryl, Michael and a

few others disagreed with them going over there, so they stayed at the gym. Scalp and others went on anyway. Several hours later Scalp came back with a torn shirt. Another one came back beaten up badly. It was a partner of theirs that they grew up with. He was messed up. Blood was coming out his mouth and nose. His brother hesitated about going back but some of the guys went over with him and caught some of the other guys playing ball. They ran in to the gym and grabbed one of the guys and started beating him. Another ran out side to help and a shot was heard everybody scattered.

A partner of theirs and his family moved into the city and had an outside party on their side of town. The whole crew went to the party and was having a good time. Music was playing and they were dances with the girls. Suddenly a girl screams and the party stops, one of their partners was hit and knocked down. It was on, a fight broke out and Troy grabbed one of the guys beating him. From out of nowhere one of the guys they were fighting pulled up a sickle and started swinging it. Ronald came from nowhere and hit the guy several times before he could cut Troy. Toney fired a shot at the guys and they all ran to the park and got drunk while laughing. Ronald and his cousin knew you were either a follower or a leader. They always had guys around them that took credit for something they had no part in. Wanting to have a gangster mentality but really afraid to shoot a gun at someone. It was always someone in the group that couldn't fight but always started trouble that was how a guy named Bro was. When Earline found out about the fight she talked to Darryl and Ronald, then she gave Ronald a good discipline.

The next couple of weeks past when a hot summer night at Bickford Bobby, Steve, Toe, Ronald, Boone and others were playing whole court basketball. Brax was one of the guys playing ball, he was loosing the game and started fouling everyone .He hit Boone with his fist in the chest because he was angry at the way the game was going. Suddenly it was a fight in the gym and chairs were being thrown at Brax and his teammates. Later on Toe and Ronald was walking to the house. They crossed over from Chelsea to Bethel and looked up by a house against some apartments a big tree was there. Ronald saw two figures standing behind the tree; suddenly these two people started shooting at them. They were running trying to get to the house to get their weapons. Blood was coming up the street and started running with them. Blood asked them why they were running while being shot at all of a sudden Blood pulls up a 357 magnum and Toe snatched it out of his hand and started shooting back. The tide changed they were making the people shooting at them started running. Toe was shooting at head and heart of each person but they were quick running. Several weeks later Toe and Ronald was walking to the house and stopped by to see their girl cousin Mary. Gaye another one of their girl cousin had told them Mary's boyfriend had jumped on her and blacked and bruised her face.

The boyfriend had been drinking and daring her to come outside. Ronald and Toe called him over and asked her why he would do something like that to a woman. He told them to fuck themselves and they begin to beat him senseless. Ronald kept stomping him in his scrotum until a businessman threaten to call the police. They stopped and told him not to come back around her anymore or suffer the consequences. After swallowing his own blood he got the picture. In their group was one little girl she was tough and not afraid her name was Lisa She was petite but wasn't afraid to fight any male, they knew because she was put to the test. They walked her home from time to time. This particular night they walked her home. They did the gangster walk all the way to her house because they had created the dance. They never knew that the dance would take off like it did. They took the dance to club No Name and showed it to others. Ronald and crew would go out sometime and see men jump on their girlfriends after they were drunk. They would then in return jump on the men who would beat up their girlfriends, because they saw it as their moms, sisters, and grand mothers. The nerve of the spineless and cowardly act of those types of men .

Unfortunately some people were hard learners. A couple days later, the very same guy Ronald and his cousin had just beaten up weeks ago was back with his girl cousin, which made Ronald extremely angry. Ronald came down to play cards. All of a sudden this very same guy starts to use profanity in front of Ronald's mother. Ronald asked the guy to respect his mother's home. The guy gave Ronald a strange look and continued to use profanity. Ronald grabbed him from across the table and starts to beat the guy. Ronald's mother grabbed Ronald off the guy and the guy ran to the back yard. Ronald ran behind him with a hammer, hit him with it and started to beat the guy. Meanwhile, Earline jumped in between the two in order to stop the fighting and accidentally got hit by Ronald with his hand. She wasn't hurt bad, but this caused Ronald to beat the guy even more. Ronald stopped because his mother and cousin begged him to while pulling him off the guy.

The next couple of days, a girl who was dating one of Ronald's partners was looking for him. She asked Ronald if he would go with her over to another one of his friend's house. He said yes but when they got there her boy friend had just left and wouldn't be back for a while. Some of the guys was going to drop her off at home at least that was what they told her. The fact was they were going to take her to another spot and have sex with her even if that meant raping her. Ronald didn't want to have anything to do with that so he stayed there, but she begged him to go with her. Ronald wanted the girl to wait for her boyfriend and not ride with these guys. Ronald was going to have to fight these two guys because they really had it in their hearts to rape her and he knew it. Ronald saved her from being raped that day and she thanked him because he made them take her home. Ronald didn't want to fight because he was having some breathing problems and he didn't want to go to Le Bonheur Children's Hospital, even though he loved the hospital because of the staff there.

It was time for a school basketball game at Westside High against East High. The game was into the last quarter when one of East High's guard was going up for a lay up when Nod fouled him very hard and was called for it. The teams almost got into a fight in the middle of the court, but it was not over. Westside would have to go to East High to play a basketball game. Then the day came and it happened once the game was over they jumped some of the players. Toe, Alex and Ronald was hanging out at Bickford Community Center when Nod and several others came in to get the rest of the guys to go fight East High players. They asked Alex, Toe and Ronald to go help them fight. They looked at each other and said it's not our fight. Ronald went over to Alex's house and met his family. Then they went to meet Ronald's mother. Ronald was hanging out when a Vice Lord started making noise talking bad about Forever Our Love Kleeve Strong. Ronald asked the young brother to slow his role, the young man didn't hear him. Then the Vice Lord did the ultimate; he threw a sign disrespecting the Nation and Ronald grabbed him but the guy had friends with him. Ronald got to a phone and made the call. The Folks were there in minutes. Alex jumps out the car with love shown to Ronald. "Where are they" Folks asked? Alex and Ronald showed them to him. They split up to hit them from the front and back. Cocktails started flying all over the place. They went at them. Folks started hitting them with baseball bats then they ran.

Folks were hanging out in Frayser . Ronald, Larry, Duboy, Alex and a few others went into a store that had a rebel flag on it. They were told to get the hell out. Ronald and the rest of the Folks didn't like that and responded back telling them to kiss their ass. The men in the store came outside to get Ronald when they saw the rest of the Folks. The men started shooting at them, when out of the blue G pulled these two beautiful silver pearl handle 38's out of his holster and started shooting back as they all hid behind cars. That led to the rest of them to shooting at the men as well. They were blessed no one was killed or shot. Sometimes it is hard to avoid fights. Ronald wasn't always good at making the right choice. While riding in a car that Blood was driving, Darryl was in the back seat with Chester and Ronald rode the passenger side. Chester had been drinking and for some reason started to pick at Ronald. Ronald was trying to avoid a fight; Chester thought Ronald was afraid of him because Chester was older than Ronald and bigger. Darryl told his little brother not to worry about Chester, Chester then said something to Darryl in the wrong way and Darryl gave his brother the okay to beat the hell out of Chester. So Ronald told Blood to pullover. Chester didn't want Blood to stop because he knew Ronald had some brass knuckles and was getting ready to use them. Chester told Blood not to stop the car and if Ronald hit him with the brass knuckles he was going to hurt Ronald. Ronald laughed while steady asking Blood to pull over for twenty minutes. Ronald was going to try to beat Chester with in an inch of his life but Blood would not stop because Blood had seen Ronald use those brass knuckles on several occasions on his enemies. He saw the damage they caused. They finally got back to the neighborhood and let Chester out at his home. That's when Ronald told Chester he was blessed.

It was about this time that Ronald started hating two types of people; white people and police officers. Like any human being, Ronald did not set out in life looking to hate others. Like anyone his hatred developed out of fear; fear because of the injustices he observed watching white police officers creating chaos in neighborhoods far from their own residences. He was tired of watching these men harass the citizens of North Memphis. He was tired of watching white men come in from Germantown and Collierville and other far out suburbs and make money off of the tax payers of Memphis to cause harm to the very ones they are being paid to protect. In a young man, fear will eventually turn to anger and anger will be used as a driving force to gain control of what the young man feels he has no control of.

The boys from Bickford did more than pull pranks and fight the Family and the Vice Lords. Beneath the hard outer surface were typical teenage boys. They hung out with each other, played basketball, and dated young girls they found attractive at the time. One early morning, Ronald was at the bottom of the steps in the school. Suddenly, this young pretty girl came down the steps of the school on her way to the cafeteria. He couldn't let her get away. He introduced himself and he asked her name. She told him her name was Tara and gave him her number as she smiled at him. Ronald smiled. They would have a long relationship in and out of school. Whenever the Nighthawks went to Frayser, they would stop into different Apartments namely Green briar, Pershing Park, Corning Village, and Northside Manor to their girlfriends. Now Ronald was afraid of this Tara's mother, but he eventually came to love and respect her mother very much. "Mrs. Baldridge", is what Ronald's girlfriend called his mother and his mother was crazy about this young lady. Ronald went home with Tara but her mother was at work. She took Ronald up to her room to show it to him just then the door of the apartment opened, it was her mother home from work. Ronald was two stories up and thought about jumping out the window until he looked down at the jump and decided he take his chance with her mother. Tara 's mother was very nice and firm in what she was trying to explain to Ronald about being in her place when she was not home. He said he understood and apologized to her mother and left with gladness wiping his head.

During the summer of 1983, Ronald and several of the young boys in the neighborhood started working at the Naval Base in Millington. They had a good time. It was hot, so water was always plentiful. Often, more water ended up on them than in them due to water fights either on break or at the end of the work period. Their jobs were Basic Beautification cleaning up Naval Base Road was a regular. Sometimes for the fun of it they would watch the Marines march as they flirt with some of the women on base. Ronald got to know his commanding officer which was a Navy Seal that from time to time taught him ways of hitting people on their body to injure and kill them . One day, while working at the base, Ronald overheard one of the guys talking about a girl he had met from the Manor in Frayser. Ronald realized after the dude said the girl's name that he was talking about Ronald's girlfriend. Through that conversation, Ronald figured out that this guy was going to be meeting her next Saturday night.

Ronald devised a plan. She had lied to him and said he was the only person she was involved with. Some people tend to play with others emotions, which is a bad idea.

He called his girlfriend up and told her he would have to cancel the routine Saturday night date. The girl acted as if she were disappointed about the sudden cancellation, but was basically okay with it. Ronald and his cousin Toe went over to the Manor and Ronald was about to knock on the door when suddenly he noticed a familiar car. It belonged to the guy from the Naval Base. The windows were all fogged up and Ronald could only imagine where the steam was coming from. Ronald could see his girl friend kissing and hugging this other man. Then he noticed a hand was rubbing all over the girl's breast, only this hand did not belong to the guy she was kissing. This hand belonged to a third party in the back seat. It was more than Ronald could stand. Kinda of high off of alcohol Finally, Ronald tapped on the window.

The girl looked astonished. Ronald told her to get out of the car and she did. The two men that was in the car also got out. They were about to jump him. They did not know that Ronald was carrying a concealed weapon. The two men were approaching Ronald, which was exactly part of the plan. Ronald, after all, wanted to blow their heads off. Ronald reached behind him and grabbed his gun from the back of his pants. He pointed it at the two men and pulled the hammer from the gun back. He was just about to shoot them when from around the corner came a friend yelling "Lizard" after him. This friend was able to stop Ronald from shooting these two men. Again, lives were spared and so were injuries, for the most part anyway. Ronald asked his girlfriend if she really loved him but before she could say yes Ronald hit her across the face with the butt of his pistol, busting her face open and causing it to bleed. He then snatched all the gold necklaces he had given her off of her neck and threw them in the park. He did not let her go until she apologized to him.

Snatching chips, fried chicken, drinking drinks, and eating ice cream in the park was a routine of theirs. They had used these methods many times. Taking the idea of the unknown Comic that use to come on the Gong Show with a paper bag over his head . They too would do the same thing put paper bags with holes cut out of them as they snatch food, chips, and other party favorites. The winter came and it snowed. Ronald and Toe decided to cut class that day to hang out. They walked up by the park and saw Michael and Rob. They jumped into the car and went to get drunk. They ended up downtown in a mess of snow. Cars were stalling, slipping, and many of them needed help pushed up the hill and out the streets. Ronald and his cousin loved to sit around and chill unfortunately it was rare. They would walk out to their cousin house in South Memphis and yes sometimes they would get into fights at the Kansas Apartments.

Many fights and near shootings would occur throughout Ronald's high school year. Ronald was certainly no stranger to violence or weapons and he was not afraid either. The older Ronald got and the deeper into gang activity he got, the more invincible Ronald believed he was becoming. Until 1984, Ronald had never actually shot at anyone, at least while in both the Night Hawks and Gangster Disciples. Truth be told, Ronald first fired a gun at the age of 12, but he had been fortunate enough not to have ever had to shoot anyone, but in 1984, that record changed at a house party in Hurt Village. One night Toe, Ronald, and Fred were over to Toe's girlfriend and a knock came on the door. They were eating and relaxing in the place. Some of the Night Hawks had came over they needed their help the Family was on Beale Street and got into an altercation with them .Toe, Ronald, and Fred didn't understand why they didn't handle the problem.

They wanted them to help them, they agreed to go to Beale Street and fight but this was it. When they got there the place was packed. They were separated for a moment except for Toe and Ronald. They caught up with some of the Family. Ronald and Toe knew that they were all together unfortunate it wasn't true. There were about 20 members of the Family, Toe and Ronald was surrounding by the Family without a word Toe looked at Ronald and they went back to back ready to fight. Suddenly the Family realizes who they were and thought they had guns on them because they slept with them, guns that is. When they caught up with the rest of the guys and asked them what happen one of the Night Hawks tried to take cheap shot at Toe. Ronald snatched him back from getting hit; they would settle this another time. Ronald and Toe couldn't believe what had happen .Toe was walking through the cut too get to his home and they were waiting for him to jump him. Toe saw one of them and hid out while doubling back going to his house. Earlier that week they had gotten drunk while walking out to Frayser they liked to do that from time to time and they found a 357-magnum bb gun. They kept the gun they had found.

Toe got to the house and called Ronald to tell him what had transpired. Ronald grabbed the oak stick and the BB gun. They met up at Bickford to handle the problem. Ronald gave Toe the oak stick and they went to fight. They all faced Ronald and Toe it was 4 against 2 but the two cousins didn't care. Toe smacked one with the oak stick while Ronald and the older brother was fighting. They thought the gun was real and that they were going to shoot them. Instead Ronald hit the older brother in the face with it and went to hit him again with it and the gun broke into. The fight ended with it settled.

Some time had passed Toe, Ronald, and Fred was in Bickford Community Center practicing for a dance contest at Lester Community Center. The day came for them to go the contest. Melvin dropped them off at the gym. They were in a room working on their steps when in walked about twenty guys from that area. They heard that Toe, Ronald, and Fred were Nighthawks and gave them an ultimatum stay for the contest and get a beaten of a lifetime or leave with their lives. They looked at each other and realized they can fight another day just not with those twenty guys right then so they walked home quickly. Some of the Family had come to Westside to get revenge from what had happen to one of theirs. The principal ran them out of the school and Toe and Ronald took another bus home to make sure nothing happened to Toe's girl friend. When the rest of the Nighthawks rode their regular bus home. The bus pulled up and from everywhere the Family came. The bus door opened and Harold starts to swing a crutch at a couple of them, while others got off the bus fighting them. Besides that, one of the Family had pulled and fired an unloaded gun at them as a prank.

Hurt Village was a housing project in North Memphis. Being from North Memphis, Ronald, his cousin, and the other Night Hawks were all very familiar with Hurt Village and knew most of the residents of this project. Unfortunately, the Family also was familiar with Hurt Village and frequently traipsed the yard of that project. Toe was dating a girl over in Hurt Village, and in fact this girl had given birth to his child. Toe wanted Ronald to the hospital to see his new little cousin. Ronald held him in his arms; he was so tiny, cute and looked just like Toe. Toe needed a car seat for the baby. They were walking just then they saw one for him. It was in the back seat of a car. Ronald took a brick and hit the window breaking it as Toe watched out. Then they took it to his baby's mother. Ronald and Toe went to attend a house party at Toe's girls house. The party went fine and everyone had a good time. Ronald and Toe left together, but walked in separate directions. Ronald and his family had moved out of Bickford to another part of North Memphis, so he had to walk in a different direction from Toe. On that evening it was hot outside some members of the Family tried to jump his cousin. His cousin took out running and fortunately was able to outrun them.

As soon as he made it to the house, he telephoned Ronald and told Ronald what had transpired. Ronald and his cousin both conspired to retaliate. They decided that they were going to go to Hurt Village exactly one week later. They say keep your friends close and your enemies closer. Ronald and his cousin both followed this general rule of life. They knew exactly what the Family was up to and where they hung out at. They knew that the Family would be at Hurt Village on any given Saturday night, and they were right. One week later Ronald and cousin dressed in all black and tucked sawed-off shotguns in the sleeves of their jackets. The Family arrived, as predicted. They both split up and surveyed the area, however no Family members were anywhere to be found. Suddenly Ronald heard his cousin shout, "Lizard, Lizard, there they go, there they go now...across the street". Ronald immediately wanted to open fire, but was told by his cousin for him to wait until they got closer. "Wait until I say now", his cousin said. Ronald's chest was beating with adrenalin in anticipating for what was about to happen. Deep down, Ronald was longing for what was about to happen. Some of the Family members spotted them before the word came and started to run. Then came the words he had been waiting for "NOW!" Ronald and cousin both started shooting at the members of the Family that were present. They took off running and Ronald and cousin followed them on foot, spraying bullets as they ran. No one was killed, but several Family members were injured. This was the first time Ronald had ever injured several people at one time with a gun. Ronald again hard headed and worrying his mother. Hoping things in the streets didn't get back to her, but this was family.

For two weeks after this incident, Ronald and cousin both were on the run. They tried to get out of the city, but it seemed every exit was blocked. The police were looking for these two extensively. "Armed and dangerous", the wanted posters read. They were forced to lay low in Frayser and other parts of North Memphis.

Finally, exactly two weeks after the incident at Hurt Village, his cousin decided he was tired of running. He wanted to go home, so both Ronald and his cousin, who had been partying and drinking at a club in Frayser for the biggest part of the night, went home tired, drunk, and somewhat overwhelmed.

The following Sunday morning found Ronald and Darryl watching TV. Doll had already left the house, leaving her two boys behind. A knock came at the door. It was a white man dressed in a suit. Darryl answered the door. "Are you Ronald Baldridge", the man asked.

"No", Darryl replied, "he is sitting over there", and Darryl pointed to his baby brother who was sitting in front of the television.

Ronald immediately stood up. There was no fight, no scuffle at all as the police officers came in and placed Ronald under arrest. Ronald surrendered peacefully, not surprised that any of this was taking place. Ronald was surprised, however, that there was a block radius blocked off during the arrest with police officers and robbery agents.

It turns out both Ronald and his cousin was taken to the police headquarters. The City of Memphis and Shelby County, at the infamous 201 Poplar Avenue, or 201, as it is most commonly referred to by local Memphians.

While at 201, both Ronald and cousin were placed in a police line-up for identification. His cousin was positively identified, but no one was able to recognize Ronald. Toe decided that there was no sense in having both of them locked up. So his cousin bailed him out and Ronald was set free. Toe wanted Ronald to watch out for his girl and his newborn son.

As soon as Ronald was free, he was out on the streets. In years, time on the streets he was making a thousand dollars every three hours selling drugs. On the weekend they sold alcohol and clothing from trades made from boosters. It was a dangerous life sometimes he slept with one eye open with his hand on his gun. They had a closet full of any gun they wanted, thanks to the streets. Up early in the morning to get a hamburger and jungle juice at a store across the street from them, Ronald, Darryl, and Blood was used to Caucasian men in big trailer trucks coming from Arkansas and Mississippi and cars stopping around the corner with African American men and women getting out to buy their drug of choice. To the going down of the Sun, they would come with ways to sell their drugs without getting caught. So they would put the drug of choice in old cigarette packages, in matchboxes, in foil and drop them on the ground in their view at all times. They would get paid, as the buyer would pick up the drug from the ground. Others attempted to do as they did and would get caught by the police. One day Darryl, Blood, and Ronald was sitting in their house rolling up a thousand joints and decided to start playing jokes on the customers that didn't have all the money to buy their choice of drugs. Blood, Darryl and Ronald would tell them to go to the house and throw a stupid hand sign to their supplier Deb, and she would know what to do. They didn't believe anyone would go and do as they had said but many of their customers went to her so much that she came to the house and asked Blood, Darryl, and Ronald what was going on.

Ronald, Darryl, and Blood fell out on the floor laughing. He made so much money in one day with eighteen-wheelers stopping by to buy drugs after making their runs that his brother stopped working at the Airline and started selling drugs with them. No matter how much money they made Earline didn't take any of the money. She kept telling Ronald she raised him better than that. Ronald thought he was helping his mother all the time he was hurting her making her cry worrying about them at night praying for them at times. Ronald and Darryl just didn't want their mother to have to need for things and wanted to take her out of that type of life style. What does a young son do when he loves his mother so much that he is willing to make wrong choices not knowing or caring about the consequences, especially when there is no strong male role model to mentor him? Ronald would remember those things he missed as a young boy without a father to fight his battle for him, show him how to break down a car and repair it. Too see a man go to work and come home to his wife and children on a daily basis. He didn't want to make another child go through those types of feelings. With an old Jolly Royal cap with some brass knuckles fastened on the back, Ronald headed out to look for his partner Alex with Duboy, Larry, and Boone while his cousin was locked up. However, they could not find Alex, another one of their partners. They decided to go over to Manassas High School where Alex often hung out. There was no sign of Alex, but they did see another cat named Jim shooting hoops in the gymnasium. He was obviously trying to impress this girl that was watching him. Jim, Larry, and Duboy decided to join Jim out on the court. One by one, each of the other boys shot a basket with no objection from Jim. So, Ronald decided to take a turn and so he joined the other four out on the floor. However, when Ronald grabbed the ball and tried to make a shot, Jim began to curse and disrespect Ronald openly. You see, some of the guys from around North Memphis wanted to be Gangster Disciples. Jim was one of them. Little did Jim know that the guy he knew as Ronald was actually Lizard from the Gangster Disciples and unfortunately for Jim, he found out a little too late. Jim tried to apologize to Ronald, but Ronald was not hearing it. In a matter of minutes Jim felt the hard end of those same brass knuckles Ronald had fastened to his Jolly Royal cap. Jim felt the hard end of those brass knuckles multiple times and with each blow came some skin off the face from Jim . Finally, Ronald saw a gold necklace around Jim's neck that he wanted, but about that time Jim had gathered his senses and struck out running. He was running as hard and as fast as he could, when suddenly he heard the whistle of the train approaching the intersection that divided Scudder Field where Jim lived from Manassas High School. Jim tried with all of his might to beat that train, but he failed. Ronald approached him, snatched the necklace and walked away without a further exchange of blows.

Within what seemed like a matter of hours, Earline had a court summons for Ronald when he came home. July 3 found Ronald sitting before the judge trying to contest an assault and battery charge for beating up a boy at Manassas High School with brass knuckles. That would not go in his favor, in fact the Courts bound Ronald over to the adult County jail. Back where he was once again in jail, you would think he'd learn a lesson but no not Ronald. Ronald called on one of his gang brothers who was holding Ronald's money for him to come and bail him out. You see, when you make large sums of money selling drugs, you can't just go and deposit the money in a savings account without alarming the FBI and Ronald knew that. This is especially true if you are a minor. Mrs. Baldridge, for whom the money was originally intended, refused to have anything to do with this so-called dirty money. So, Ronald had to rely on a couple of guys he'd trusted with his life at times to hold his money for him to save in an account from selling drugs. One of these individuals was a cat named Blood, the others name was Der.

Ronald called Blood to see if Blood could bail him out of jail. There was a problem and this problem could not be discussed over the phone. There was no money. Ronald was highly upset and was thinking while he listen to Triple 6 and M. J. G. with 8 Ball . The 4th of July was around the corner and Ronald wanted to be out to enjoy the festivities. This did not change the fact that Ronald would not be out in time, unless he could get someone else to bail him out. He called his mother and with a fake promise (a lie) to not get into any more trouble with the law, Mrs. Baldridge bailed her youngest son out of jail. Because of a mother's love for her children they are willing to loose everything.

Come to find out, Blood had not spent Ronald's money. Der another man in the drug game that they got their drugs from Deb husband spent the money. They thought they could trust him to hold and save their money.

Instead Der spent their money paying off his drug cases. Der promised he would pay them back but in drugs, not their money. That meant they would have to sale all the drugs to get back the money they should have had. Ronald didn't want to go back on his word to his mother not to get into any more trouble with the law. However, desperate times meant desperate measures. Ronald could not allow this other person to spend his money. Ronald wanted to get the guy and make him pay them back. Ronald and Blood needed money and they needed it fast. They needed a plan. They were desperate.

Desperation. Desperation will make you do some funny things. It will make you risk your life. It will cause you to make decisions you otherwise would not have made. Ronald could not have known that desperation was about to make him do something that would change his life forever. Ronald and his brother started getting very close

Left To Die

July 7, 1985 came and Ronald had developed a plan to restore some of the cash he had recently lost. Their plan involved robbing a place of business in the Frayser community. They had got a tip from the disc jockey that worked there. The night came, Ronald saw another ex girlfriend named Gloria. Something didn't look right in Ronald's eyes and she wanted him to come and talk to her. Ronald refuse here that opportunity. Another person drove Ronald, and Blood to the destination, while others watched out. Blood was going to make sure the security guard was out of the way. Ronald was to take care of robbing the cash register. They staked out the place in order to keep an eye on it. Once the man they identified as the manager stepped away to count the money, Ronald and Blood made their moves. The guard comes to his car for some strange reason. Ronald and Blood ran up on him, Blood shot the guard he went down. Ronald heard a second shot and thought Blood had took care his part. Ronald ran into the skating rink while Blood headed around to take care of the security guard.

Ronald snuck up on a young female, grabbed her by the hair and shoved the barrel of his gun in her mouth. Ronald then told the manager to put the money in a bag. He couldn't have known that Blood had run off without taking care of the security guard. Suddenly, the security guard appeared. A nervous and surprised Ronald went to point his gun at the security guard, but the security guard was able to aim at Ronald first. Suddenly shots rang out and that was the last thing Ronald remembered.

Recovery; Wheelchairs, Graveyards, and Jail Cells
Memphis, Tennessee
1985

Paralyzed instantly by the bullet that entered Ronald's back, Ronald's breathing was getting shorter and shorter. Ronald was sure he was going to die in the back of this ambulance that was carrying him to a nearby hospital. He barely prayed a prayer of forgiveness because he knew something had went wrong and he was dying. He was fighting to breathe. He attempts to get up but can't move. He heard sirens coming but laid there. Meanwhile the security guard stuffed money up under Ronald's body to reassure the justification of him shooting Ronald in the back. Ronald could neither move, talk or try to tell what had happened. The paramedics start to cut his clothes away and work on him. They lifted him up and put him in the ambulance. The young policeman got in. He looked over and saw a Caucasian police officer who was riding next to him. Ronald asked the police officer if there was any chance of surviving while the paramedics speeding through the streets of the city of Memphis

on their way to The Med. The police officer, which Ronald would later come to know as Officer Steve Grisham and eventually just Steve, said that Ronald would survive, even though he himself was not too sure. At that moment Ronald began to lose oxygen. His body stained with his own blood, fighting to breathe while praying inwardly. The police officer that had stayed by his side began to pray for him. The officer sitting with a hand on top of the young black gang banger's hand knowing a mother is somewhere hoping her son is alive. Ronald handgrip weakened and heart had stopped completely again. Ronald saw a very bright light at the close of his eyes as he laid on his stomach.

In the meantime Ronald's mother, brother and a friend of theirs were out looking for him. They looked in dumpsters, garbage cans, and allies. All the while Doll just prayed her son was not dead. Together the three searched for Ronald from 11:30 p.m. until 7 a.m. the following morning. They ran into Blood and asked Blood if he had seen any sign of Ronald. Blood lied and told them no.

Discouraged and frightened, Doll and Darryl headed back to the house. Suddenly a knock came at the door. Doll had a feeling that bad news awaited her on the other side of that door. She opened the door to find a circle of police officers. As she digested the news about the fact that her youngest son was in the TICU on life support at The Regional Medical Center (The Med), she collapsed into one of the officer's arms. All of a sudden the police chief told an officer to arrest Darryl and bring him in for question. Earline couldn't believe what was happening. Her youngest son in the hospital fighting for his life and her oldest son possibly arrested for nothing. Blood was there at the house as well, so when the police took Darryl in for question along with Blood and several others. Darryl was worried about his baby brother and his mother. One of the Caucasian police officers that Darryl and his brother had seen get away with breaking the law and rules in their neighborhood passed him by knew them. Just then Darryl asked the policeman "where was his brother"? The officer responded to him and said, " your brother is in surgery and I hope he die". Darryl looked at him with tears in his eyes. They started to question Blood and some of the others. Some of them started to talk including Blood about what they knew. Blood told on himself. The police released Darryl. His mother was there to pick him up. All the while Earline was at the police department trying to clear her son so they could go and check on Ronald at the hospital. Meanwhile the staff at The Med went to work on Ronald doing their job. The two of them with Earline's sister by her side hurried out to the hospital to see Ronald. She saw her son laying there, Darryl with tears in his eyes, as he felt helpless. Her little son, his baby brother what had Ronald done. Earline kissed Ronald and whispered in his ear "be glad you're hurt, I'd *beat your ass*". When Earline and Darryl got back home they noticed their door was open. Someone had broken into their house while Earline checked on Darryl and Ronald.

Everyone in the neighborhood was upset about Ronald's situation. They could only think about the times they had spent together. These guys had been through a lot together. They grew up together, played football together, played basketball at Bickford Community Center together, laughed together, cried together, played together, and fought together as children. And after they finished fighting together, they laughed and played some more. They went to dances together, both at school and the clubs.

Once Ronald did become conscious, he could not talk for an entire month. He had to write down everything he wanted to communicate on a sheet of paper. The nurses and doctors were constantly poking him with needles and checking his vital statistics. Blood gasp three times a day, suction tubes in his throat, on heart monitors, a respirator to breathe for him and in constant pain. Not able to eat solid food so Ronald started to loose weight this continued for three months. When Ronald first became conscious and started communicating by writing, one of the first things he indicated was that he could feel his legs with his hands, but he had no feeling in them. There was a African American nurse in the room and she asked him if he remembered Teddy Pendergrass, an R & B singer from the 60's, 70's and 80's who was in a car wreck and lost the use of his legs. Ronald shook his head indicating that he did remember the singer. The nurse let him know that he was just like him; unable to use his legs and paralyzed from the waste down.

Ronald cried like a baby. He was angry at himself and angry with all the people who were supposedly watching his back. Most of all, he was sorry he had caused his mother more pain, grief and had hurt his brother.

Every other day the hospital phone rang with reporters trying to find out what happened. Regret, pain, and shame are just some consequences that happen when young children are abandon by their fathers and mothers. It is a problem when fathers don't take care of their responsibilities but leave a mother to raise a son without an example of what a real father is. Equally bad is a daughter that never witnesses a responsible mother and is forced to make bad choices that result in the birth of a child for which they are unable to provide for. AIDS, crack, street life of hustling, prostitution and lack of a high school education plagues their life. The boys end up dead, on crack, in prison or just like Ronald in a wheelchair.

The next night he got visits from several of his fellow gang members all strapped with weapons including the Night Hawks and The Gangster Disciples, word was sent from the city something needed to be done about this. They asked Ronald what did he want them to do to all the people that were involved. He looked at all of them some with tears in their eyes and wrote down the word "nothing". Killing or hurting them wont make me walk again as a tear fell from his face. Later that night, Ronald was awakened by his legs moving because of his injury. He started getting happy when a nurse walked over. He got her attention to tell her his legs were moving, she smiled as she held his hand and told him he was having involuntarily movement known as muscle spasms.

A few days later, Ronald began trying to pull the tubes out of his body because he was sick of the doctors and nurses poking him and sticking him with needles, not to mention in constant pain, and having to be suction out through his trachea. Bullet damage to major parts of the body along with cuts from operations was painful. One evening shift and the nurses was just coming on Ronald started choking and couldn't get the nurse on a call button to suction him out. He threw things in the hallway to get someone's attention and finally just when he was giving up a nurse came over suction him out gave him a pain shot took his vitals and smiled at him as she walked off. Ronald began imagining his new life in a wheel chair, and the thoughts were not positive. His Aunt and cousins would come by to see him and pray with him. They'd come with his mother sometimes. He pictured himself as a young man living in a nursing home. It was not the way he wanted to live. Ronald began to have thoughts of ending his life and he even attempted to pull the tube out of his neck that was helping him breathe. At this point, the nurses began to tie his hands to the bed rail. Ronald began to pray for the use of his legs for just one last purpose; to kick the nurses who were trying to tie down his legs. Those prayers were not answered. Meanwhile his brother took over the drug game and made it bigger setting up drug houses here and there with a couple of friends and family. Mean while his cousin Toe had got the news while he was locked up. It hurt his cousin Toe deeply because Ronald was shot and paralyzed in the hospital on Toe's birthday.

Within the first three weeks of being in the hospital, Ronald developed a bedsore on his backside stage two with drainage coming out of it. This occurred because he could not be moved while laying in the bed because of all the tubes that were keeping him alive. Ronald also developed pneumonia, in addition to the asthma from which he already suffered. Chest tubes in his side ribs three in the right side and two in the left side to help him breathe. All of this only further complicated his recovery. Surgery had to be performed in order to remove the bullet from his spinal cord. This was an extremely dangerous procedure because of the fact that they did not know for sure where the bullet was lodged. When they did locate the bullet, they discovered it was laying directly in the spinal cord. This injury would cause Ronald pain for the rest of his life, if not kill him. The doctors gave Ronald a 50/50 chance. "It is up to Ronald his mother said". After the surgery the first face he saw was his mother's. She smiled at him and said mommy is here, he had heard that so many times in his life. Ronald had to do physical therapy with 15 heavy staples in his back to seal the wound. This would be the beginning of a lifetime of working with pain. Ronald remained in critical condition after the first month he was at the Med. The staff there was compassionate beyond description and they paid close attention to Ronald's condition and was there for him every step of the way.

Gloria was an old girlfriend from his junior high school days. Like Ronald, she had asthma. She was loud from time to time but was crazy about Lizard. When she found out he was shot and in the hospital tears started to flow down her face. She had told him not to go anywhere that night he was shot. The next day it rained but that wouldn't stop Gloria from seeing Ronald. She and a friend started to walk from North Third Street out to the Med to see him. She saw him and started to rub his hand. As the time passed, she would come out and comb his hair wash his face and give him a stuffed animal. They'd talk about the times they had together. Even though he couldn't talk, he wanted her to know he loved her for coming to see him. She kissed him on the head and left as she wiped away her eyes. Mean while Tara, his current girlfriend, would come
out to see him as much as possible combing his hair, holding his hand, and praying for him. Ronald was awake in TICU during visiting hours. In walked Earline, his Aunt, and her daughter all with a smile on their faces trying to be strong for him. They held his hand for a while as they wiped

his face and said a prayer before they had to leave. Darryl, Darron, and the rest of the fellows didn't have time to hang out at the Club No Name to do the gangster walk. They were to busy trying to survive as others were going to jail or prison for other crimes they were being charged with. By the time things got back to normal, the gangster walk had taken off and everyone was doing the dance.

After two months, Ronald was moved out of TICU at the Med to 5 D floor where he would get to know the nurses, nursing staff, and doctors that had a great deal of compassion for him even though Ronald was angry at the world. Spivey, Bettie, Brenda, Robert, Mrs. Grove, Ms. Lewis, Richard, Mable and a host of others showed him why The Med was so very good at what they do. These men and women at the Med were special because of their compassion, love, commitment, dedication, and determination all that with more to ensure that every patient was giving their best. Ronald experienced that quality everyday he was in the Med. Every day he went to the whirlpool to clean the wound. Ronald was angry and would spit at some of the staff. One day, a new nurse named Mable came back from vacation. She had Ronald as a patient on her first day back to work. She heard he would spit on staff because he was angry with himself. Ronald couldn't talk and needed to be suctioned out from time to time. When Mable went in to suction Ronald out, she said "look little boy, they say you like to spit on folks that are trying to help you…if you spit on me, I will spit back on you". Ronald rolled his eyes and was cursing her out with his eyes. Mable said, "you can roll your eyes all you want, but if you spit on me, Ima spit back on you". Ronald never did try to spit on her and they developed a relationship that lasts to this day.

A few weeks had went by, the doctor came into the room to check on Ronald and his mother asked the doctor if Ronald would ever get the trachea out his throat. The trachea was due to the fact his lungs were weak from all he had been through. The doctor looked at her and said mother it is very possible he will have that in his throat for the rest of his life. Earline looked at her son while grabbing his hand and said we will pray about it. Ronald realized he had to do his part so he started breathing treatments and his lungs got strong. A couple of days later, Ronald wanted to talk to his mother. He had the nurse call his mother. The phone rang and his mother's voice came over it. He spoke the words " momma, it's your son, Ronald." She couldn't believe he was talking. The family came out to the hospital and started talking about things that happened in the neighborhood.

There were times when Ronald wanted to give up because the physical therapist at the Med was on his case but for the good. One particular day he had to go to therapy he was in severe pain and consequently he was angry. Although, Pam, Elleen and the others understood, but they also understood that Ronald needed to work past the pain in order to gain independence in his life. Ronald refused to work when he was in pain. When you have 15 steel staples in your back, you tend to suffer from pain. On this day he asked the therapist to take him back to his room, but she refused. It was odd for her to refuse his request. Finally, she agreed to take him back to the room if he could roll up the steep hill. Ronald told her bye and started to try to roll up the hill, but he couldn't make it up the hill because he wasn't strong enough. Ronald had gotten stronger in The Regional Medical Center and was ready for transferring over to the Baptist Rehab Center.

After a month at Baptist Rehab, Ronald needed some new high top tennis shoes for rehab. His big brother wanted that to be a gift from him .So Darryl went out and bought his little brother some Reeboks and a warm up suit. Darryl had taken over the drug game along with family and friends. Darryl had set up drug houses in various spots in Memphis, so he was making money.

He worked hard because he knew he had people that had hatred for him who hoped he didn't make it back. Ronald learned right then to never give up. To use the negative feelings as motivation to succeed from people that hated him and counted him out. They had a strict routine at the rehab center. Tara his girl would come out to visit him with her mother. Ronald however didn't want Tara to put her life on hold and thought she should go on with her life, so he begun to push her away. She deserved someone who could walk. He was up every day at 6 a.m. and was given 30 minutes to dress. After breakfast, there was a strict regiment of physical therapy that involved weight lifting, push-ups, and balancing practice. Practical lessons, such as how to catch yourself if you start to fall, were supplied. There were also lessons that provided practice in wheeling a wheel chair up a steep hill. Ronald learned how to get back into the wheel chair if he fell out and how to transfer from the bed to the wheel chair and vice versa.

After lunch was occupational therapy. In occupational therapy, Ronald learned how to cook, how to clean, how to wash dishes, and how to make a bed. Everyday life skills were taught. Much of this Ronald already knew how to do, but he had to learn how to do it all over again from a different vantage point: a wheel chair. Ronald's life would never be the same again. While Ronald was learning how to live his life in a wheel chair, Doll was going to court to try to make sure her baby boy would not have to live his life in a wheel chair behind bars. Ronald was given Bible verses from Romans 8th Chapter from his cousin Aaron, who was the pastor of True Gospel of Deliverance Church. He believed God had left him here for a purpose, but what was it? With his mother comforting him with the words of Jesus, Ronald was given faith to believe that no matter what he went through on earth, God would be with him through it all, God is faithful. What about you? What will you do with God's promises? Ronald was released to go home. However, before he could go home he had to appear before the judge in juvenile court. They rolled Ronald into Juvenile Court and there it happened. Ronald came face to face with the security guard. Their eyes met, the security guard said to Ronald "I should have killed you". Ronald smiled at the guard as he thought back to the night close to 20 gang members came to see him in the hospital to ask him to say the words to have everyone involved to come up missing. While in court, Ronald heard the white cop who had watched him flat line in the ambulance, testify against him. Additionally, the security guard from the place of business, the manager of the place of business, and the young female worker who had a gun on her only four months earlier all testified against Ronald. Ronald sat there in pain listening to testimony after testimony. He was in so much pain he could not even be afraid of the possible outcomes. All he wanted to do was take some pain medication and go home.

Instead of going home, though, Ronald found himself on the way to the county jail. At the jail, he was booked and seen by the jail doctor. Because he had three severe bedsores that had not healed due to the severity of his injuries, he was transferred from the county jail to the incarcerated section of The Med. Ronald underwent three operations to take care of his 2 three stage bedsores by a plastic surgeons named Dr. King and Dr. Hickerson. Little did they know when they met that Day they would see a lot of each other and get to know each other well. Each time for surgery Ronald would request they bring in a radio for him to listen to as they operate on him the surgeons and staff agreed to that. Meanwhile, Doll was in court trying to convince the judge to allow Ronald to be transferred from the incarcerated section of The Med to the area where regular patients were. This request was granted and Ronald was transferred. He was glad to be back on 5 D where the staff was like family to him. The staff had compassion on a young man trying to find his way back. That was just how the staff at the Med was. Meanwhile, Ronald was enjoying his freedom in a room by himself. Earline, his Aunt and cousins all came out to see Ronald to tell him the horrible news that someone had killed one of his cousins by accident. Ronald asked them did they know who did it? No one had an answer other than speculations. Ronald didn't want to cry in front of his family. He waited until they left and tears just started falling down his face as he reminisced about the fun times he had with his cousin.

After the final surgery, Ronald was allowed to go home. Ronald had to appear again in criminal court first. This court date was set for a week after he was released. Before Ronald went to see the attorney he read earlier from his mother's Bible in 2 Kings 20: 1-5 where God told Hezekiah get his house in order he was going to die but Hezekiah turn his face to the wall while praying with openness and honesty. The Lord spared Hezekiah's life and gave him 15 more years. If it worked for Hezekiah it will work for him Ronald, he thought. He began to pray "God I don't know you like I should, but I'm asking you to deliver me from this trial." The criminal court prosecutor offered Ronald ten years in the state penitentiary. They thought that because so many had testified against Ronald, that it would be an open and shut case. There were some questions about how some of the money was found on Ronald's body which was suspicious, like money found in his pocket, money up under him when his hands was out in front of him to keep from falling hitting his head, and the guard swore he shot Ronald because Ronald shot him which was not true. They would later find out in court that the bullet the doctors got out of the security guard was not from the gun Ronald had. The judge that was overseeing the case in court didn't want to further try the case in his court, so he had the case transferred to another courtroom. They asked Ronald and Doll if they wanted to accept the prosecutor's offer. They refused. Ronald was given a public defender by the name of Gerald Green.

The evening on the night before Ronald was to appear in court, Doll called him into the living room. She told him that she was going to beg the judge to let her do his time in the state penitentiary. Ronald kissed his mother on the cheek and told her no way would he let her do his time. Ronald's mom told him if the courts convict him. Earline didn't think her son needed to go to prison after going through what he had been through at that time. Their attorney was a young public defender with a practice on the side. Finally the time had come for Ronald, and Earline to go see the attorney. The state offered him ten years in a prison while in a wheelchair. Ronald knew he had been through enough but there wasn't much he could do. They had all the evidence against him. With the other people testifying against him in court it looked bad for Ronald . Including the white policeman who rode with Ronald in the ambulance on the night of the shooting. Ronald remembered that this white police officer no doubt would remember with vivid detail that Ronald had put a gun in the girl's mouth and held her hostage.

It was at that moment that Ronald understood the real meaning of a mother's love is to priceless not to appreciate her. His mother told him again if he lost the case that she was going to ask the prosecutor for the DA could she do his time for him. Ronald hugged his mother tight while crying. He knew how much she loved him but he could never let his mother do his time. The evidence was against him. Nothing left to do but trust God. Sure enough the Lord God would show up. The day came for the ruling on his case. The Public Defender Mr. Green came over to Ronald and his mother and said, "don't smile, grin or show any emotions. The court is getting ready to dismiss the case against you." Ronald looked with awe on his face because God had shown him that he answers the prayers of those with true faith. Mr. Green was glad for Ronald.

A New Life Thanks To My Enemy

1985-1987

Ronald left the courtroom happy. Ronald went home and thanked God for His mercy. He tried to do right. He started hanging closer to home and not in the streets. However, home seemed too much like a jail cell. Being in a wheel chair did not help. Some of his so called friends stopped coming over and people stopped calling. Ronald's girlfriend at that time would come around, but Ronald pushed her away. The Nighthawks and Gangster Disciples were still there for him and Ronald would not get out the gang just yet. That's right Ronald was gangbanging in a wheelchair. Ronald began rolling his chair around outside. He started out wheeling a short distance and gradually went further. He would wheel up and down

North 7th Street. Friends and family would see Ronald wheeling himself in rain and extreme heat, blow their horn, throw up their hands, and keep on rolling. Ronald began to recognize how much his life had changed since being in a wheel chair.

One change Ronald did not expect was how people would test him just because he was in a wheel chair. Some of the same guys Ronald grew up with and went to school with began to test their limits with Ronald. Additionally, new guys coming into the hood also wanted to mistakenly think that just because Ronald was in a wheel chair that he was a weak punk. Ronald found himself having to prove them wrong.

Ronald couldn't allow himself to give up so he would push his wheelchair where he wanted to go. He had to show others that the only thing he couldn't do was walk. Some of the same guys he fought with side by side including family members of Ronald stop coming around. Michael, Steve, James, Alex and a few others got together from time to time to barbecue and joke about when they were young with Ronald and he would remember that. There were others that he grew up with and hung around that felt because he was in a wheel chair he could not be used anymore. Ronald would see them out somewhere and they'd blow their horns and keep going. It didn't bother Ronald; he understood it was time for a change. At some point in life you have to want to change for the good in order to make a difference. That includes leaving those people completely alone to better yourself.

Ronald started getting calls from some of the sisters in the Gangster Disciples. These were some of the same young beautiful ladies they used to get their targets in the open. You see when the Gangster Disciples were trying to get someone they would get one of their sexy sisters in the gang to get next to them to lower their guards and then boom! The gang was still there for him he would not turn his back on the gang. So, Ronald went back to gangbanging in a wheel chair because whenever he had trouble from anyone and went to FOLKS. If he needed help they would be there to offer aide and assistance in minutes. Ronald believed in keeping his secret silent, remembering what the symbol the crown and the six-point star meant. Ronald understood the King David Boxdale, Hoover and Shorty Mack concepts of getting as many young African American men and women under their leadership to vote, despite the violence he knew would occur within the organization. There was a problem however rogue and false flagging gang members that were misleading young children. They realized that five thousand voters backing them, gave them a voice to make a difference. If only all the gangs could get together, help talk to the youth, help curve crime and change things, what a powerful voice that would be.

Darryl and Ronald would sit up and talk at night about everything. His brother would come get him and take him to a house. They would sit and listen to music. Marvin Gaye was one of Ronald's favorites until his brother turn him on to David Ruffin. They started to get close again as they talked about dreams and goals.

One afternoon of wheeling in the streets, Ronald came home to discover a surprise package came in the mail. In the package was a check of $1648. It was back pay for social security. He split the money between his mother, brother, and himself. He took what was left and put it away to save.

As he was counting the money later that night with his cousin that played basketball for Westside High, a knock on the door came. Now Ronald and this cousin had been drinking earlier that day. On the other side of the door was Bay; a guy that had went to school with Ronald back in the day. Bay was notorious for starting fights that he could not finish. Bay spotted the money and challenged Ronald to a game of dice for the money Ronald and his cousin were counting. Ronald agreed to play gamble; if he lost he wanted his money back. Bay agreed to these terms. So, they began to shoot dice. Ronald lost instantly. Ronald held his hand out to Bay for his money, and Bay looked at Ronald, looked at the money on the bed, and snatched the money off the bed. Ronald snatched Bay, grabbing him by the shirt collar. Bay hit Ronald in the jaw and as he was trying to get away from Ronald, Ronald grabbed the sawed off shotgun he kept under his mattress and hit Bay with the barrel of the gun. Bay dropped some of the money and a couple of his teeth came out. Bay ran out the door and Ronald placed the gun under his leg and wheeled out behind him. Bay was running and Ronald was rolling and eventually Ronald caught up to Bay. He stopped in front of a dope house and Ronald shot him in the head. A car pulled up and some of the former gang members from Ronald's past got out. Ronald gave them the gun, wheeled back to the house, turned the TV on, took off his shoes, popped a top on a beer and acted like nothing had happened. Earline had come home; Darryl

came behind her with an associate of his.

About ten minutes later another knock at the door came. This time it was Officer Steve Grisham, the white police officer who rode in the ambulance with Ronald when he was shot. Officer Grisham informed Ronald's mother that Ronald was under arrest for aggravated assault and he arrested Ronald. Officer Grisham placed Ronald in the back seat of the police car, put his wheel chair in the trunk, and drove Ronald to the county jail. As Ronald rode along on this short trip, Officer Grisham asked him how he was doing and later got around to asking why he had shot the other guy. Ronald explained the story and let him know it was self-defense. Officer Grisham did not question Ronald any further and gave Ronald his card with his home telephone number on it.

Ronald was checked in at the county jail and stayed there until the court date. On the second floor, in the L part is where he met a guy named Tony who had two broken ankles from a jailbreak-gone bad. The two got to know each other. Ronald a gangbanger, Tony Vietnam vet with a robbery charge. Tony wrote the Sheriff a letter on Ronald's behalf for him defending himself. On the day of Ronald's hearing, he was given a $1 million bond. Apparently there was some confusion at the jail. The jail personnel made a mistake and thought that Ronald was still serving time from the robbery two years before in 1985. Ronald had to call his lawyer, Mr. Green, to straighten out this matter. Attorney Green came to the jail and got it straight. Bay confessed that he had indeed tried to rob Ronald in his own home. Ronald was then released.

Later that night, Ronald decided he needed to do laundry. As he was cleaning out his pockets, he came across the card that Officer Grisham had given him earlier. Ronald heard a little voice inside saying to give Steve a call. Ronald picked up the phone and called Steve. He offered to take Ronald out to dinner and said he wanted to talk with him. Now being a young man, eating was one of Ronald's favorite past times. So they went to an all-you-can-eat buffet. As they ate and talked, it amazed Ronald how much this man could eat considering he was of a small build. Now at this time, Ronald did not know that this was the same officer that rode in the ambulance with him after the shooting in Frayser that landed Ronald in a wheel chair. Ronald didn't remember that this was the same officer that testified against him in juvenile and criminal court.

As the evening went on, Steve began to remind Ronald of his past. Ronald was shocked to learn that this was the same cop who had seen Ronald at his lowest, weakest, and worst. Steve told Ronald the events in detail that transpired on the night he had been shot in Frayser . Ronald let the police officer know that he was planning to sue the security guard at the skating rink and the company where he worked. Steve did not think this was a good idea, but Ronald was determined and Steve's opinions at that time were of no concern to him. Steve drove Ronald back to his house and came in to meet Mrs. Baldridge. When Ronald told his mother who that man was, she just looked stunned. She wanted to know what this man wanted with her son. Ronald told his mother that he initially thought Steve would question him about the other gang member, but that topic did not surface. Ronald had a difficult time believing God would forgive him for all the things and sins he had committed. Steve would take him to 1Corinthians 5 all that is in Christ old things has past away behold he is a new creation. 1st John 1:9 if you confess your sins he is faithful and just to forgive and cleanse you from all unrighteousness and John 16: 24 hitherto you have ask nothing in my name, ask that your joy may be full. These were just a few verses Steve gave and quoted to Ronald to assure him of his salvation.

A couple weeks later, Steve asked Ronald to go to a youth facility with him to speak to some young offenders. So, Steve, Ronald, and a guy named John "The Bull" Bramlett rode to Somerville, Tennessee. John was a retired NFL player who had played for the Miami Dolphins. Steve and John were both members of Bellevue Baptist Church. That was the first time Ronald was able to speak to a group of young people. He couldn't know that this was the beginning of what would be his career for life and the beginning of a beautiful friendship. During their drive back to Memphis, Steve asked Ronald how he liked speaking to those kids. Ronald said he felt high…high like he had never felt smoking marijuana. They both laughed about that.

Steve and Ronald began hanging out together. They would go out to eat, drive around the neighborhood. They spent time with each other's families. Steve began to show Ronald things about his own neighborhood that Ronald had never noticed. Ronald began to realize that this man, this white police officer, was a friend and a mentor. More and more Ronald began to travel with Steve to different places to speak to young offenders. Each time Ronald loved it more and more. One night, while Ronald and Steve were out driving around the neighborhood, Steve asked Ronald if he would like to go to church with him. Ronald said he would like to do that, but he did not have the proper attire to wear to church. Steve let him know that was not a problem. Steve took Ronald out and bought him $100 worth of clothes. Ronald began to get suspicious of Steve's motives. However, Steve never asked Ronald about any of his former gang friends, nor did he ever ask for any of the money back that he had spent on Ronald. Little by little Ronald dropped his guard around Steve.

One Sunday, Ronald was listening to Dr. Adrian Rogers, the pastor of Bellevue Baptist Church, preach. When the alter call came, Steve asked Ronald if he wanted to go down to the alter? Ronald said he did not want to go down at that particular time. Finally, one Sunday Ronald nudged Steve and said he wanted to go down to the front. Ronald unlocked his wheelchair and Steve pushed him down to the front of pastor Adrian Rogers. He shook Dr. Roger's hand and told him he wanted Jesus to be his savior. On that day, Ronald became a Christian. He was scheduled to come back the following Sunday in order to be Baptized. Ronald was hesitant because he did not know how he was going to get in the baptism pool in his wheel chair. Steve and the pastor assured him that they could accommodate him.

It was time for Ronald to be baptized at Bellevue Baptist Church. They had him get into a wooden chair and they tied him securely in it. Then they wrapped a sheet around him in the chair. Once everyone else who was scheduled for baptism had been baptized, Steve and Dr. Rogers both picked up the wooden chair that held Ronald and baptized him in the name of Jesus. He was excited to have changed his life with a new start. Ronald was tired of banging, shooting at people, and being shot at in a wheelchair was getting him nowhere.

Not long after Ronald's baptism, he got very sick and needed to go into the hospital. While there he was rolling down the hall and over heard two people talking in a hospital room. It was the mother of a young woman who asked her why didn't she get out the room more and make friends. The young lady responded that people don't want to make friends in here. Right then, Ronald backed up to her room and said to her he would be her friend. They exchanged numbers and names. This was the beginning of Ronald finding his first girlfriend since being paralyzed. The two of them got out of the hospital and kept in touch. They went out together and got to know each other very well. In fact, she was not like a lot of girls Ronald had run into since being in the wheelchair. She didn't stare at him with strange looks. She was not afraid to ask him questions about the chair. She would come and pick him up and they went out to eat or to the movies. There were many occasions when they went out together and she would get tired of walking, she would sit in his lap, put her arms around him and he'd roll her around in his chair. Going on picnics was a favorite of theirs. Not long afterwards, Ronald got a major infection with a high fever and needed to go to the hospital again.

This time Ronald's mother was there in the hospital room with her baby son as she rubbed his head with a cool towel. Holding his hand was a must. You know there is something about a mother's touch. In walked his girlfriend with concern on her face .She came to give his mother Earline a break.

Earline went out to get some water for Ronald and take breaks as the nurses and doctors gave him medicines to bring down the fever and infection. Ronald went to sleep and awoken to his girlfriend in the bed holding him. Ronald moved then she woke up with a smile on her face. He squeezed her tight and told her how beautiful she was. She smiled at him and said she knew she was. Time passed and he got strong enough to eat food, plus his fever went down. Ronald got well and left the hospital.

Several months had past and they were still acting like two little lovebirds. Staying up on the phone waiting for the other one to hang up . Ronald had to go out of town on business for a week. When he got back in the city he had a dozen roses, a bottle of champagne and a card for her as a token of his affection. He was excited to be home because he wanted to see her very badly. He made a phone call to her home and her mother answered hello. Hello he replied, and Ronald asked to speak to her daughter. She was still hurting, he could hear it in her voice as she told him his girlfriend had gotten extremely sick from Lupus and they tried to contact him but failed. Ronald couldn't believe what he was hearing. The next day he went to her gravesite and left the roses there. Later he got drunk listening to Marvin Gaye *Distant Lover* at the house while looking at her picture with tears in his eyes.

Don't Get It Twisted

One such incident occurred in the summer of 1988. Darryl had been shooting basketball with some of the guys. Darryl had on a bracelet that he did not want to get broken. So, he took it off and had one of the guys hold it for him. After the game, Darryl asked for his bracelet back. The guy who had been holding it did not want to give it up. Instead, he tried to charge Darryl $10 for holding it. Darryl, knowing the bracelet actually belonged to Ronald, went and told Ronald what was happening. Darryl didn't want to start a fight or a shootout if he didn't have to.

Ronald and Darryl went and found the guy to find out what the problem was on his end. The guy who had been holding the bracelet told Ronald that he wanted $10 for holding the bracelet. Ronald let him know quickly that no such exchange would take place. "You better give me my damn bracelet back or there will be problem", Ronald said.

Immediately, Toe, Ronald's cousin who had been Ronald's closest cousin, friend, and confidant, jumped in and said to Ronald "he aint got to give you nothing". Ronald dismissed them and rolled away with Darryl at his side. Darryl didn't want to fight he wanted to avoid trouble but couldn't at times.

Two weeks later Toe and some of the same guys who had been on the basketball court earlier when the bracelet incident went down, were all gambling in Bickford Apartments. Ronald and a friend showed up to try to retrieve the bracelet one last time. Ronald pulled out a 357magnum gun, pulled the hammer back, and told them not to move. Ronald began to look for the guy who had his bracelet. Ronald looked over his right shoulder and saw the guy crossing the street, as if he were trying to sneak up on Ronald.

Ronald fired a shot at the guy. The guy fired a shot back and everyone who had been gambling scattered. Ronald started shooting at the guy in the middle of Bickford Apartments. Finally, Ronald and his friend escaped without injury. One week later the dude who had Ronald's bracelet came to return it. However, the friendship and family relationship that Ronald once shared with his cousin Toe was never the same.

Eventually they would have to put their differences on hold. David, Toe's younger brother, was awesome in basketball. David stood an even 7 feet tall and he was making his family and all the guys he grew up with proud of him because he was playing basketball, which was all of their dreams. He started playing at Westside High School, and then he went on to play at Texas A&M University. He later got a good paying contract to play ball in Straussburg , France. When he had signed a new contract from his team, he bought his wife and family some things and himself a new sports car. The word came while David was driving his car he lost control of the car and drove off a cliff several feet down. There they found his body crushed to death. The family was in awe. All the teachers, coaches, friends, and family members could not believe he was dead. They had a closed casket funeral for the family. The basketball team didn't want to ship his body back to the United States so Westside 's coach Z and David's family had to contact Congressman Harold Ford Sr. to help get his body back to the United States and they had his funeral at the Ford Funeral Home where he was put away very nicely.

A few months later Toe and a couple of his boys were hanging out when gunshots started flying. A friend of Toe's came out of nowhere blasting a 12 gauge while Toe started shooting back. Some of Toes enemies came to rob them .Toe got hit in. The bullet went straight through his body. Someone contacted Ronald to inform him of what had happened. Ronald called Alex and Folks because he wanted to go see his cousin in the hospital at The Med. They entered the room and there Toe lay in the bed knocked out on pain pills. They wanted to know who did it .He couldn't say at that time. Ronald called John, a young brother from the hood. You see Ronald knew when he needed to handle business. John, Alex, Toe, Ronald and a few others didn't mind shooting it out with anyone, including the police. In time they would find out who shot Toe and it would be taken care of.

Here We Go Again
This was the point where Ronald began to realize that life is truly about choices. Darryl his brother was taking care of business setting up drug houses, getting bulletproof vests, and making money-selling drugs.

Ronald had to have a check up; Duboy one his associates along with his mother and cousin who sat in the back took him to the Med. Duboy was driving suddenly it started raining on the way home. They made a turn down Avalon off Poplar while it continued raining. Duboy told everyone to hold on the bakes were going out, he made a right to miss a car coming toward them. He had to make a quick left to keep from hitting the two men on telephone pole.

The car went left and Ronald door came open and was thrown out the car. He hit his back and rolled up in the yard of some people. His mother came running, crying and calling his name. She held his hand with tears in his eyes and threw a blanket over him to keep him warm until the ambulance got there. They took him back to The Med. While he was in the hospital in pain on a heart monitor, an IV in his arm, bandage head, arm, and leg. His Aunt, his cousin Jimmie, her son and his wife was there before he knew it seeing how he was feeling. He got a knock on the door .It was Steve he looked concerned and prayed for Ronald because he couldn't stay, he had to go to work. Steve made Ronald laugh with a joke. Steve was becoming more than a mentor, he was becoming a friend. They had to put a rod in his right leg because it was broken. That meant another operation. Ronald weren't too happy about that. When the time came Earline, Darryl and his sisters would be the first his eyes would see, two weeks and he was back to rolling. Time past and an infection was set up in his leg and the rod needed to be removed. Ronald had an infection osteomylitis, which caused him to have to take several bags of antibiotics. He had to be taught how to mix three different types of antibiotics and administer the 326 bags of medicine into a Hickman porter cath to his chest connected to a main vein of his heart.

Darryl his brother would stop by Ronald's place to see if his little brother was okay. Earline didn't want her son to go through this by himself. Ronald was truly grateful and loved her dearly but he needed to do this by himself. He told his mother she could go home, that he needed to take care of that himself .She was upset but understood , she kissed him on the head and went home. Ronald told her she would not be here all his life and he needed to do things for himself. Ronald got better and started going back outside. This is when things started looking up for Brother Ronald. Ronald wanted to go back to school but didn't know what to do. His cousin Aaron introduced him to Tony. Tony went to work to help him go back to school to get his GED. While at the hospital for a check up a nurse asked him to visit with another young man that was paralyzed. He was a former Vice lord that was shot several times; he needed someone to talk to. They reached out and introduced themselves. "Mervyn is my name what's yours"? "Ronald is mine".

When Mervyn got out the hospital they went to a spinal cord meeting. The two became friends; the both of them went to GED classes because Ronald believed he owed his mother that much. They both were in constant pain from their injuries. Tony, Ronald, and Mervyn the three of them would get together on several occasions to play wheelchair sports like basketball, baseball, para sailing, and rugby. Eventually they would start speaking in schools, churches, parenting seminars and other places talking about consequences of choices. They'd travel up ad down the road together going fishing in Brownsville and Nashville, to heading up to Tony's hometown in Kentucky for a ham festival. They thought it was funny, you see walking they probably would be at each other's throat. The wheelchairs drew them together. They both saw the path young people were going down in Memphis was the wrong path and even though there were some pastors of churches out on the battle field Ronald wondered where were the rest of the churches and pastors. He knew the severity of the problem and how it was going to escalate. Ronald and Mervyn believed this way, when they were banging they were dedicated so why not be dedicated to the Lord and to saving as many young people from making the choices they made. That, however, would come with a price because they knew there would be people who wouldn't like that. Sure some people was on their side but it was Ronald and Mervyn who had to deal with guys threatening their lives because they were enlightening these young people who were forced into gangs, bribed, threaten, peer pressure because they couldn't fight for themselves, and picked on. Because long gone were the days of daring a child to knock a stick off your shoulder or drawing a line in the ground telling them to cross it. Children today just shoot their guns.

One Saturday early that morning some of the ladies and gentlemen in their spinal cord support group got together and went fishing in Brownsville. They met up with some of their other partners from Nashville. They were having ball in the heat trying to catch fish and win a trophy. Ronald was one of those people that didn't care too much about the fishing as he did the time he spent with friends. People he understood who had the same code of ethics. Needless to say Mervyn was on a roll catching fish. He came with most fish caught. They all finished up and jumped back into the vans and came home. Early the next Sunday morning the phone rang. "Hey Ronald, it's Tony", the voice on the other end of the receiver said. Tony had called to give Ronald some bad news. One of their friends that they went out of town with fishing was run over and killed that same Saturday night by a drunk driver. Ronald couldn't believe his ears. They had just seen each other laughed, joked and played around, but it was true. The following weekend about 20 wheelchairs rolled up in the church to see their friend for the last time. Ronald often wondered when his time would come because he knew what he saw when he died.

Ronald went back to his old gang members, both the Gangsta Disciples and the Night Hawks to call a round table meeting. Ronald wanted to tell them that he wanted out of the gang. He was tired of being shot at, fighting in clubs, shooting at others and chaos in general. He wanted to tell them that he had a life-changing experience and he was ready to drop his flag. They asked Ronald to leave the room so they could vote. The gang members voted unanimously to make Ronald an inactive member 1991.

Ronald was hanging out at Bickford one day when one of the guys got angry with Ronald and called him a handicap bastard. Ronald was still growing but still had a ways to go. Suddenly, out of Ronald's shirt came a snub noose 38 and shots rang out from Ronald shooting at the guy. They got into a shootout in the parking lot of Bickford. Finally Ronald needed to get out of there because the police would soon be there. Some of his associates came driving by and saw Ronald. They opened up the door. He jumped in the car while they broke down his wheelchair and put it in the trunk of the car and drove off. The police came but no one said anything.

Along the way Ronald started meeting people in wheelchairs with various back grounds from gang bangers to former military (special forces), diving accidents, car wrecks, and etc .The beauty in it was they didn't see color, they saw wheelchairs because whatever affected one of them in a wheelchair affected all of them in a wheelchair. People don't care or have any compassion just because you are in a wheelchair. Ronald found the compassion and empathy he needed from his wheelchair bound kinfolks. This extended family stuck together in all matters. If Ronald had a problem, all he had to do was make a phone call and before he could explain the problem, those friends were on the way.

1991 My new family

Ronald later met a home health nurse who came out to see him. Her name was Candy. She was quiet but knew her job. She would have this big smile on her face. One day she came to visit him and she introduced her self this time. They became very good friends; she then introduced him to her beautiful friends Jeanne, Mary Martha, Judy, Linda, Donna and the rest of their families. Ronald was introduced to Jeanne's brother Sonny. He was a good man with a big heart that loved the Lord. Ronald and Sonny had something in common. They would get together for breakfast and have Bible study sometimes. They would hang out at cookouts, basketball games and baseball games with Sonny sons sometimes. In fact they would get together on Christmas and it was lovely. It was as if God was giving Ronald new family and friends to replace the old ones, that's the way he is. Candy and Jeanne came over with Mary Martha while she was in town.

Earline and some others didn't understand their relationship. Four Caucasian women pushing a young African American man around in a wheelchair at the Mall of Memphis, restaurants and movies looked strange to a lot of people, but it didn't bother them not one bit. One day they wanted to take Ronald to Little Rock to see television evangelist. Ronald mother Earline was not sure about this trip. She didn't want anything to happen to her son. The women promised Earline they would take care of him. The morning had come for them to leave for Little Rock.

They loaded up the cars with bags of clothes and water, food, and other things they all needed. They finally were outside of Memphis, when Ronald called home to reassure his mother he was okay. Finally the drove to the Little Rock Coliseum to see this world renowned television evangelist .The music started at the revival and most of the people with handicaps and disabilities were put in the back. Ronald wanted to be close to his friend's .The only way he could do that is to get out of his wheelchair and sit in a regular chair. Ronald was hesitant about leaving his wheelchair but he'd take a chance because Candy and the rest of the women said they would watch out for the wheelchair.

He sat in the chair with his sisters. Darkness came over the stadium and the television evangelist came out in all white and started talking. Praise music was playing in the back ground as they started to worship. Ronald watched as the television evangelist asked his followers to stand up and half the arena stood up. In one of the moments in the crusade when it looked like the television evangelist got caught up in the moment or spirit and swung his suit coat at a man that they brought up on stage and hit him. The man rushed at the television evangelist with his fist balled up and security rushed him off the stage. It was kind of funny to Ronald. Another point in the crusade the television evangelist told the crowd to stand up and hold hands. He said he was going to blow into the microphone and the spirit was going to knock them down and they would be filled with the spirit. Ronald figured he was sitting down anyway the holy spirit would pick him up but nothing happen to Ronald when he blew into the microphone other than people pulling each other down. Ronald kept his eyes on his wheelchair until the lights went off.

When the event was over the lights came on and there was no wheelchair. Ronald looked and laughed as Candy and the rest of the women went looking for the wheelchair. There were wheelchairs everywhere just not the one Ronald and the girls were looking for. They just grabbed one with hopes they would get his back. They were more concerned about what his mother was going to say. On the way back home they were trying to figure a way to tell his mother what happened. They got to the door, his mother looked at him then at Candy and Jeanne for an explanation. They told her they were very sorry and would do what they had to do to get his wheelchair back.

Candy, Jeanne and Ronald called the phone number on the wheelchair, someone answered the phone. They asked did they have a certain wheelchair in their possession. They said yes and they made arrangements to get the chair back. Mean while back at home Ronald had problems getting in the bed so Earline called Jeanne and Candy to tell them he needed help getting in the bed. Phillip got up out of bed at 1pm in the morning to help Ronald get into the bed. A few days went by and Phillip met the person with Ronald's chair in a safe location to swap out the right wheelchair. Earline would later forgive the women for losing his chair because she came to learn that they loved Ronald like a little brother. Candy, Jeanne and Mary Martha would spend many days together doing different things like cookouts, birthdays, holidays and church. Meanwhile on days that Ronald wasn't in constant chronic pain he would volunteer at non-profit organizations mentoring at risk teens and talking to spinal cord injured. Helping the teens make better choices and spinal cord injured recover to become as independent as possible.

I Can Do All Things

Ronald started to make a difference in the lives of young people. Ronald had a new friend named Dan. Every weekend the two of them would get together and leave the city for some R&R. They'd take a three hour trip to Little rock, Missouri, Alabama and other places in Tennessee. Ronald often times would go rolling it didn't bother him to push his chair where he wanted to go. Ronald went places in his wheelchair that people wouldn't go that could walk. This day it was hot outside and Ronald went rolling .He went through a short cut to get to his destination Bickford Community Center. Just then a guy was following him. Ronald stopped to see what was the problem . Right then the man pulled a gun on him and told him this was a warning from a certain gang. Ronald grabbed the barrel of the gun with his hand and the gun went off shooting Ronald in his left hand. The bullet went straight through and people came out, as the man ran. One of the neighbors in the apartments called the ambulance. They came and took him to the Med were the doctor gave him an x-ray. The doctor took some saline water with a big syringe tube and pushed it into Ronald's hand to clean it out. It burned and Ronald hand started hurting but the doctor wanted to make sure everything was okay before he gave him pain meds. Finally the doctor asked him how it happened and Ronald told him. The doctor eyes got big because he had never heard that before.

The doctor gave in a shot, and then sewed up his hand. The doctor told Ronald to keep his hand elevated in the arm cushion sling he had on. Ronald's mother almost lost it. Her son had been shot again. Ronald went for months with a cast on trying to get around. Opening doors was very difficult for him. Not to mention putting on his clothes, and trying to push a wheelchair. People didn't care about the fact he was in a wheelchair with a cast on his left hand when he was out somewhere. The day finally came to have the cast removed Ronald was so glad because he experienced how people that could walk could be so ungrateful. They always complained about something even if it was small issues. Ronald wouldn't have to struggle to open doors any more when he was at the doctor or somewhere else. The people normally walked on by as if he wasn't there. He saw first hand people were blessed but had no compassion for others including themselves. Weeks went by and the hand healed back to normal again. Ronald realized he needed to be very careful next time and not slip up. Ronald remembered who sent the message and he would send one of his own back to that person.

When I Die Have No Pity Bury Me Deep In Gangster City

One night Ronald got a phone call. It was a partner from prison, Ralph. They spoke; "what's up family how have you been"…"fine", Ralph said. I need your help". "Sure what's up family", Ronald replied. "My cousin is in a gang and he along with some other young brothers are being misled", Ralph explained. "I've been talking to them but I'm in here and they are out there", Ralph continued. Ronald said, "I'll help but I'm not coming back to the gang." Ralph just didn't want his cousin to end up in a jail cell, graveyard, or wheelchair. Ronald went to talk to the young brothers in a park. There were about ten of them. Ronald asked each of them what they wanted to be in life. No one said a word. Ronald helped them to see that life is about choices and they had to be wise with the choices they made. He explain to them how Jesus plus education equals success. He went on to explain that the literature gangs have is about the positive but if someone is teaching the opposite then they are to be watched. Because not even a true gang banger would want their child to go through what they have went through if they truly loved them. The sad part about it was that there were older gang bangers or those wanna be that were misleading those young brothers and sisters. He had to explain to the young girls who wanted to be down in the life of gang banging what it really was about. He explained that King David had Queen Sheba for the girls to fall under. The male gang bangers were blessing in young girls through sex which was on many occasions was raped. One of the strictest codes in the gang is that we are to protect, love, and respect our parents and elders because they pave the way. The job of the men was to protect their sisters and women because they carried their future seed and legacy. The young people started listening, but a problem arose. A certain gang leader wanted all of them to join his function. The young people didn't want to but were afraid to say anything to the gang leader. One evening, Ronald was watching television while it was raining. He was in a lot of pain and he had just taken a couple of pain pills. "Hello", the voice said, "I'm Mrs. Johnson and I got your number from a church member and I need your help with my son". "Sure", Ronald said, "How can I help you"? "My son runs away from home a lot and is some where downtown…I have a young child that I can't leave and I don't have a car…can you help me please?"

Ronald drove over to the woman's house. She gave him her son's name and a picture. Ronald made a phone call to his friend Mervyn. They met up downtown at each end of Beale Street. Mervyn spotted the boy and gave Ronald a call. They met in the middle. Officer Grisham was downtown with his eyes out for the boy as well. Ronald and Steve on the same side trying to save young boys against ones like Ronald used to be. A former gangbanger and , a Policeman working together…, but to Ronald that was just a glimpse of what the city of Memphis could become if everyone could work together. They talked to the boy and he talked to his mother while they drove him home.

Ronald was working out in his place another day when the phone rang. It was one of the ten young gang bangers Ronald had been mentoring. They had gotten together to ask Ronald to go to the gang leader on their behalf. Ronald had a friend that worked at the community center in the neighborhood that knew all the children from that side of the street because he grew up there. Ronald decided to ask this gentleman to watch his back. They use to play basketball against each other as teens. North Memphis had a lot of young boys who could play basketball back in the early 80's. There were very few people that had the guts to cross Chelsea Avenue to come to Bickford in North Memphis back in those days as teens in the late 70's early 80's. This gentleman was one of them. So, Ronald knew he was talking to another soldier like himself from back in the days that would shoot it out if it came to that. They talked about it. They agreed for him to watch his back. Ronald never told the gentleman that his younger brother was one of the young men he was trying to save from making the mistake of joining the gang and that he didn't want to join.

Before Ronald did anything he stopped and prayed for help from God. Ronald knew what these young brothers could do. You see he was going to talk to a gang leader that wasn't known negotiating. Ronald flew a kite, which is symbolic of a letter, to a very good friend in prison just in case things went bad. Ronald wanted this friend to know the details of the negotiation that was about to take place. Ronald let him know who he would be talking to, where the meeting would be, and what the purpose of the meaning was. The call from the friend in prison came and so the meeting was a go. They would meet in the park in two days. Ronald went to the park in the area they were familiar with. The gang leader came with fifteen soldiers for security.

Each gang member with a gun in their pants was on post looking out for the police and everyone else. No one entered the basketball court. The gang leader knew Ronald as "Lizard". They spoke out of respect. They sat and talked about the reasons the gang leader would benefit from having these young men under him. Ronald asked him if he had any children ? The gang leader said yes and Ronald went on to ask the guy would he allow his children to go through what he has been through. The struggle wasn't over. Ronald asked the gang leader has he ever gotten shot or died. Ronald said to the young brother that he believed in the youth. Ronald remembered all the things people had said to him as a teen. So many had counted him out but he was still here for a purpose. Ronald went on to say how he hoped to see the young people he talks to, mentors, or works with succeed in life. Those were his plaques and trophies. The gang leader told Ronald get to the damn point and Ronald said, "I'm willing to die for these, our most precious pearls, our youth". Ronald asked the gang leader what would he give up for them ? The gang leader let the ten boys go free. A few months later that very same gang leader kills a guy in a park in Memphis because the boy hung with Vice Lords, a rival gang. The boy was used as an example. The police found a headless body in the park that was shot off with sawed off shotguns. The gang leader wanted to send a message to other Vice Lords in that area. The police locked the gang leader, along with several other young gang members for the murder of a young man. A life taken away just because of whom he was hanging out with . What about you? Who are you hanging with and will it cost you your life?

A couple weeks later, Ronald was pushing his wheelchair down the street when three men from the gangster disciples stopped him. They asked him his name and he told them. Right then one stepped in front of him and told him that they saw him on television. Another one went on to say what he was doing wasn't cool...trying to get boys out of gangs. Ronald asked them which one of them want their son or daughter manipulated into doing wrong and then caught to be thrown to the sharks referring to (the prison system). We are supposed to show them the right way, not the wrong way, and that they are the future. One of the gang members stepped in front of him and held out his to shake it. Ronald didn't know if he should shake his hand or not, but he shook his hand anyway. Then Ronald watched the three men walk off.

Several weeks later, some gangster disciples he knew very well visited Ronald. A young woman in her late 20's was with them. Ronald was curious why she was with them until she told him she was a sister. She went on to tell him how she became one. She said her mother told her to go to school, but her boy friend called her and told her to come to his place. She went over to his place and they started to have sex. When he got up off of her, the door flew open with about ten guys around the bed. She asked them what they were gong to do to her. The boys pulled down their clothes and started to rape her. She told the story to Ronald with tears in her eyes. She begged, pleaded, cried, screamed, and even promised she wouldn't tell anyone, but no one came to her aide. In fact, when they finished raping her from 7:30am until 2:30pm, they said, "welcome to the nation." That's right that could be someone's daughter, sister, cousin, or mother.

Ronald went to a church that same Sunday in that week. When he got there he noticed all the handicap parking was gone. He had saw this all to much people paying someone to get them a handicap placard so they could park in the handicap parking. It amazed him because he knew a lot of them weren't handicap nor did they have anyone with a disability in the car. He saw a spot so he went to park when a deacon stopped him from parking there saving it for a woman. Ronald laughed at the hypocrisy of these people. He wondered if maybe that's the reason so many people that say they are believers can't reach people who are hurting from various problems. African Americans always complain about how bad Caucasians treated them, but as soon as they got the chance they do the exact same thing, they did. Were the people in church more concerned about material gain instead of faith in Jesus? Could it be true that like the Bible speaks of in the last days the love of many would wax cold? *(Matthew 24: 12 And because iniquity shall abound, the love of many shall wax cold).*

Mean while, another day came and went. Ronald was speaking at a Memphis City School and a teacher asked him if he ever met this Chaplin that worked with gangs in prison. Some people had been trying to get Ronald and the Chaplin together for some time, but at that particular moment their paths had never crossed. However, that was about to change in an unlikely way.

The Tears Of A Mother's Sons

Ronald was getting ready to get on the van with a friend one afternoon when his mother asked him for an Alka-Seltzer. She then started complaining about her chest, so Ronald called the paramedics. The paramedics showed up just in time because his mother collapsed to the floor as soon as the ambulance pulled up. They rushed in and went to work on her. They put her on the stretcher while Darryl was coming around the corner. Their whole world had stopped. No one really can prepare for a love one to pass and this was their mother. Ronald was pushed into The Med hospital in a hurry by his brother Darryl while trying to find out the location of their mother. Earline had a heart attack and would stay in the hospital to have a triple bypass surgery. The day come for the operation and there her family stood in prayer for her to come through; her older sister, nephews, and nieces all standing around her. She got out of the hospital and started to recover when a close friend of hers got sick at the hospital from Asthma. Earline wanted to go, but Ronald didn't want his mother to go. In the end, Earline got her way, but Ronald went along with her anyway. Within a few hours of arriving home, Earline called Ronald complaining about chest pains. Ronald called the paramedics. Darryl, Ronald and a friend rushed to the hospital. The doctors wanted to keep her for observation. They kissed her on the fore head and told her they would be back to pick her up tomorrow. When they left, her eyes rolled back into her head and her speech slurred from a stroke. The doctors tried to contact the two brothers to inform them of what happened.

When they returned to see their mother she was in a coma. She remained for two weeks. A young cardiologist came over to Ronald and Darryl to discuss their mother's prognosis. Neither one of them were able to hear him from shock of seeing their mother laying there so helpless. With tears in their eyes they asked when and how? The stroke had occurred within five minutes of Darryl and Ronald leaving the night before. They immediately called the family. Earline remained in the hospital in a coma. Darryl and Ronald were at the hospital every visiting hour to see their mother. The doctor constantly tried to get them to pull the plug saying she would be a vegetable. During that time, Ronald put his whole life on hold including mentoring young boys. Ronald would get up in the morning praying and go to sleep praying for his mother. He started to remember he was partially to blame for his mother worrying about he and Darryl. Ronald and Darryl were driven to visit their mother in the hospital by Sonny with his son. The doctor came in and showed them an x-ray of their mother's brain and how it was black. Sonny's son grabbed his leg and started to cry. Sonny hugged his son with tears in his eyes because they all had become friends. Sonny asked the doctor was there any chance for Earline coming out of coma, the doctor replied not by all the x-rays. Ronald and Darryl almost had to threaten the doctor's life to leave the idea of taking her off life support alone.

At the end of the week, Earline's sister Mary Ann came to Memphis. Girlie and Mary Ann went to the hospital to see their baby sister alone. The time would finally come that the doctors wanted to talk to the entire family. That morning came too soon for Ronald and his family. Ronald had a friend that went to the hospital with him. Horry and Ronald met while Ronald sat on his porch and they spent countless hours hanging out, drinking coffee, and laughing and joking. Horry was a Christian and he and Ronald often visited each other's churches. He was walking by and remembered Ronald went to Manassas High School. Horry had gotten to know Mrs. Baldridge very well, as well, and he was extremely hurt and saddened by the news of her current condition and thought it was wise not to bother Ronald with more bad news.

The place Earline's family was going to meet with the doctor was a room next to Earline's. Everyone made it up stairs before Ronald. He pushed his wheelchair into the hospital corridors where there was to be absolute quietness. Ronald heard a lot of noise coming from his mother's hospital room. He got nervous while rolling into the room. Darryl, his brother, came over to him and put his arms around Ronald. Ronald still had no idea what was going on. Darryl told him to look at his mother, Her eyes were open. She had come out of a two week of coma with a smile on her face. Ronald rolled over to his mother and grabbed her hand and asked her did she know who he was. She smiled and shook her head trying to say yes to him. God and his son Jesus had heard their family's prayers, once again. The young doctor came into the room in shock, as he said he couldn't explain it. He didn't know what to say. According to the x-rays she was a vegetable; no state of consciousness, no feelings or awareness of any thing. Right then Mary Ann said they knew where it came from. It was from the Master, referring to Jesus and Jimmie along with the rest of the family second that motion.

They prayed and gave thanks to God for his favor and went to see Earline. Earline, however, would have a long road to recovery. Ronald and Darryl prayed day and night for their mother to recover. Some time we can be so selfish wanting our love ones to live on in pain, suffering just to satisfy their family. Ronald and Darryl saw the road she would have to take. Smoking for those many years, along with the stress in her life all added to her condition. She would not want to go on in that state of condition. Her two sons did not miss a day at the nursing home where she was to get rehab until she got better. The strain of trying to regain what she had lost would take a lot out of her and she was tired. Ronald went up to see his mother and had a talk with her. She said she was tired, and he understood what that meant. He had been through that himself. Ronald remembered the words she would tell him when he was shot and in the hospital paralyzed. John 14, *Let not your heart be troubled.* She smiled at him as tears fell from his eyes. He told her thank you for all your love and she was the only mother he ever wanted. No woman would take her place and would she forgive him for all the pain, sufferings, tears, and heartache he caused her. Earline smiled and gripped his hand and said yes. The next day Darryl went up to see his mother and talk to her about things.

The following day Ronald woke up early and called out to the nursing home to let his mother know they would come see her at 2:00 p.m. The nurse put her on the phone and she said nothing to him. Ronald started to talk her; meanwhile different people were trying to connect Ronald and this Chaplin together. Ronald had no idea his last words would be to his mother "remember, mother, Jesus died for you that you would live and die for him with your faith in him". The nurse said she looked sleepy and that she was going to put her back to bed. Meanwhile, Earline never said a word.

The time had come for Ronald and Darryl to go see their mother when the phone rang. The person on the other end asked them to come out to the hospital for their mother. Earline had passed away in her sleep. Their whole world stopped. Ronald and Darryl were in a great deal of pain, hurt and feeling a void. It felt as if the world had gotten a little colder and the people a little crueler. From out of nowhere a phone called came. It was, Chap, the chaplain from the men's prison. He told Ronald he would see him at his mother's funeral. Ronald didn't believe he would show up, and he was in too much pain to care at the time. Ronald and family called their cousin Aaron, who was the pastor of a church, to conduct the funeral service. The service was held at True Gospel Church of Deliverance. Ronald looked up and much to his surprise he saw Chap sitting in the pulpit. When the funeral was over, Chap came to Ronald and told him to take his time they would talk. Steve sent flowers and came by to see Ronald and Darryl later that night. Meanwhile, his sisters Candy, Jeanne, Mary Martha and others would check on them and let them know they were there for them. Ronald was grateful to have friends such as those.

For a long time Ronald could not grieve. Trouble was on the rise like locust. Ronald saw on the news that gang activity was starting to increase throughout the city. Ronald called Chap and they met the next day to talk at lunch. They discussed how they could handle the problem. Chap told Ronald he knew some other men that would want to help. The next couple of weeks Chap introduced Ronald to Gates. Chap wanted especially to get the Nation of Islam involved to help because of their prison system reformation program .The men realized they all had something to bring to the table and each of them were putting their lives on the line, that they would be caught in the middle. On one hand they wanted to stop the gang problems from increasing with the crime and violence. On the other hand there were people that had no knowledge about what gangs were. Some people would make it tough and possibly not listen to them because they weren't apart of a click. They went on to pray about the situation. In October Ronald got a call from Chap. A group of congregations of churches wanted Ronald and Chap to be facilitators to 300 children and teens about gangs. Is it possible that some gang signs are demonic or satanic? Some of the youth asked them that question in group sessions because of the horrible crimes that were being committed. What would you do if you found out a close friend that was a Christian had AIDS from a tainted blood from a transfusion and was dying? That's what happened with Ronald. His friend family called Ronald to inform him about his friend. Ronald's friend thought Ronald wouldn't be able to handle it. Ronald went to visit his good friend as he lay in the hospital bed dying. There wasn't much Ronald could say to him other than to quote John11:25-26 *I am the resurrection and the Life he that believeth in me, though he were dead yet he shall live; and whosoever liveth and believeth in me shall never die. Believest thou this?* Then his friend reached out his hand to Ronald. Ronald grabbed his hand as a tear fell from Ronald face and his friend smiled at him. Ronald stayed as long as he could. Ronald later learned his friend had passed away before he could see him again.

Standing For Something Sitting Down

Ronald and Chap broke up the classes into two groups. Chap started stacking to show young people he knew what he was talking about. Ronald took another approach. He started talking about his life; the reasons why he tried to justify selling drugs, gang banging, and teen violence. He talked about the all the pain and hurt he caused his mother. Then he asked them how many were hurting the love ones trying to raise you the best of their ability? None raised their hands; Ronald could see the look of regret on their faces. They both talked about the serious problem of young girls having children by boys that were not ready to take the role of father hood responsibly. Ronald asked the young men to remember what it felt like to go without a father teaching them how to repair a car, how to fight, or have a man to defend them against bullies. Ronald looked out into the crowd and saw young men with tears in their eyes. Chap and Ronald knew where they were coming from. They, too, had been down that road a time themselves. Sometimes Ronald would help Chap out by speaking at his Exodus program on the military base with Judge Joe Brown and others.

From time to time he would get the chance to grieve and remember his mother. He had lost another woman he had loved and decided not to get to close to people. He would remember in speaking to say to the children to love their parents, guardians, and those that took time out from their lives to try to make the best for them.

He missed his mother very much; the First African American Queen in his life.

A couple of his friends wanted to do something to cheer Ronald up, so they talked him into going to Columbia, South Carolina, and spend some time with them on the river of Fort Jackson Army base. Ronald didn't have a problem with going, it just happened to be two weeks before Christmas. They struck out driving and finally, after 11 hours, they made it. It was too late to go on the base so they stayed at the Governor's House hotel not far from the base. It was cold there but beautiful. Ronald enjoyed fishing, hanging out on the base learning more and more about the base. The time had come for them to leave and the weather outside had changed drastically. The wind coming off the river and the temperature dropped to 20 degrees wind chill of 17, you couldn't beat Ronald jumping out his wheelchair into the jeep on their way back to Memphis.

Ronald was asked by a young mother to help her son get out of a gang. The leader of the group was trying to force the boys to sell drugs, show them how to rob, and steal cars or suffer the consequences. The young boy was 12 years old and Ronald needed to know where the young man lived, what his name and alias were, where he hung out, and what type of car he drove, if any. The young boy gave Ronald what he wanted to know. So Ronald called chap to inform him of what was happening just in case. Meanwhile Ronald had met several new brothers that were gangster disciples that believed in what Ronald was doing. Through negotiations, Ronald was able to successfully get the young brother out of the gang.

Ronald decided to call Mervyn to see if he wanted to hang out. Mervyn answered his phone and told Ronald he was hanging in with his girlfriend. So Ronald went out to a nightspot to shoot some pool and watch the game on TV. Ronald was trying to get by a man's foot. He asked "the man could he move his foot please". The man looked at Ronald and said no go the other way. Just then some one bumped into Ronald causing him to roll over the man's foot. The man got up and started talking very loud to Ronald. Ronald took a look at the man and smiled, while reaching. Just then, about five men surrounded Ronald and the man. There were several gang members, which no longer gang banged, in the club. A hand touched Ronald's shoulder. It was a gentleman that had read in the papers about what Ronald was trying to do. They also were talking to young boys on the street about gangs, voting, and education. These men were from various gangs that included the Gangster Disciples, Vice Lords, Crips, MS 13, Jamaican Posse, and the La Raza. Many of these men had gone back to College and became Lawyers, doctors, computer specialist in special fields and law enforcement. Ronald introduced himself to the men and they started talking. One the men told Ronald perhaps they could work together to stop this problem. Some of them had degrees in education and law. Ronald was glad to have more help. He had prayed for it, due to the fact that Ronald was in a great deal of pain from all the injuries, operations, and broken bones.

Ronald returned home and he checked his voice mail. There was a message on the phone asking him to come and speak to a group of teen boys in a mentoring program. He called them back the next day to get the time, date, and give his okay. While on the phone, Chap told Ronald to be careful. While Chap was out emptying the garbage a couple of Crips tried to do a drive by and shoot at him. Just then another call came in from prison telling Ronald to watch his back. Some gang members were going to try something stupid for revenge. Ronald made a phone call to Steve to inform him of what was going on. Steve gave him some numbers to gang task force, where he had friends that would help Ronald when needed.

During the summer of 1997, Ronald started getting requests to come speak in churches, parenting seminars, community centers in other cities more and more. Ronald's brother Darryl decided to leave Memphis and travel. Ronald was up late at the house studying a hunger report. He and some others were to arrive in Atlanta Georgia for a hunger coalition conference and he was one of the keynote speakers. While down in Atlanta, Ronald and a couple of friends headed out on the town when he got a call from his brother Darryl in San Diego, California. Darryl wanted to let his brother know his location and where he was working. Ronald had to be back in Memphis soon. Promise Keepers event was coming to Memphis and Ronald looked forward to hanging out with his good friend and landlord Robert. That would be an emotional, reviving, spiritual boost the both of them needed. Robert thought it would be good for Ronald to go and it was. Ronald saw thousands of men from various backgrounds, cultures, and from across the country singing, holding hands, and praying together. It was a small glimpse of what the world be like if they could all come together.

Meanwhile a couple of days later Ronald was asked to be one of the facilitators at The W.D. Kalian Center for parents. Ronald tried to encourage mothers to challenge their children, because he saw on the regular how bright and intelligent these young people were. They needed some guidance in the right direction. Ronald challenged the men that were walking. Surely, they wouldn't let a man in a wheelchair that had chronic pain, and muscle spasms that volunteered at Caldwell School working with the students as a tutor, out do them in the area of community involvement.

One day, in 1998, an associate was talking about trying to get Ronald to join the APO division at Juvenile Court. He thought about but wondered what would they think about his past. Ronald went and filled out an application for Auxiliary Probation Officer. Chief Brown would be his interviewer. Ronald didn't know what to think since he was in a wheelchair. A former gangster disciple with a badge now ha! ha! Ronald met with the director Bobbie and second in charge Denise.

He was a little nervous because he was the first person to ever volunteer for their program in a wheelchair. Ronald joined the Go Team Division 10. They went everywhere to see a child in trouble, from city to county. They were amazed that Ronald could do the job even in severe pain. Ronald first case he had to take a mother's children from for inadequate housing. In 1999, they gave Ronald a surprise award for outstanding service. Ronald was happy but really enjoyed it when a child he helped came and thanked him. There would be many children that grew up as young man would stop him on the streets and thank him for his help.

Ronald tried to find out what his probationers liked to do. He would take them to baseball games, football games, to the Memphis Grizzlies games for good behavior when they made good grades in school or do something to respect their parents. On the flip side he would take them to

The Regional Medical Center (Med) emergency room, jails, graveyards of young people their age, as well. He would show the youth the guys he grew up with and they saw how they were hooked on crack with no place to live and he'd show them bullet wounds on his body so they would get the understanding about the consequences of choices. After all, Ronald had lived two different lives. He knew what it felt like to walk, what it was like to sit down in a wheel chair, but the ultimate goal was the third life; to live walking in paradise with his Lord, brother, mother, friends and family.

Ronald loved the APO program plus mentoring young boys of single mothers in schools. Ronald got a call from an elderly mother and father. Their son was getting into all kinds of trouble at school at the Middle school at South West Tennessee Community College. Ronald went over and talks to the boy. He asked the boy his name and he said Caleb. From that point on the parents, Caleb and Ronald came up with some guidelines to help get him back on the right road. Ronald would see him at school because the boy went to school on the same college campus where Ronald was attending. Ronald got permission from Caleb's parents to let the teachers and principals know to contact him in case Caleb got in trouble. One year later the boy was back on the right road and graduated from school. He now serves in the United States Navy with a beautiful wife and child in California. He later got the chance to say thank you for Ronald's help.

Every case was different to Ronald no matter how tough the child's underlining problems were. These problems varied from young teens running away from home, drugs, teen and gang violence. They all needed attention from their parents; someone who would listen to them, spend time understanding what they feel and the pressures of peer pressure.

The directors were amazed at Ronald's commitment from a wheelchair. Some days Denise and Bobby would talk to Ronald while he visited Juvenile Court. They saw the pain he would be in from time to time as they talked to him about his cases in the cafeteria. It was one of those things that don't kill you, come to make you stronger. This was his cross to bear for the choice he had made in the past. He learned to learn from other people's bad choices in the past and tried not to make the same choices they did. Ronald would go on to receive several awards from Juvenile Court for his service. Ronald had worked with so many organizations in Memphis along with giving them some ideas. In 2000, Ronald decided to go take classes at Shelby State Community College, now, South West Tennessee Community College, for a while on an Associates Degree in Social Work. While there, he met some interesting instructors. These instructors challenged him. He liked that they understood him, what he did and why. Sometimes he and Mervyn would come over and give workshops about gangs, teen violence and benefit for mentoring single mother's children.

Ronald decided to start his own company. He and an associate both came up with the name for the non- profit organization; P.I.A.N.O. Inc. (partners in alliance needing others) *Bringing harmony back into the lives of at risk boys by working together like keys on a piano.* .
The company was helped formed by his one time public defender Mr. Green now associate and board member of the organization. The concept came from a white policeman Steve working with black gang banger Ronald. Their mission would be to find mentors for sons of single mothers who sons were paralyzed from violent crimes and to go into schools to speak to students about the consequences of bad choices. These

mentors became friends with those in wheelchairs going through tough times like depression or just to have someone to talk to that had been in their situation. There were certain staff members at a hospital in another city that was concerned with treating patients that were gang members in fear that their friends would come back and harm them. They contacted Ronald and asked him to come in a give a presentation on gangs and how to treat them. The associate left the organization, leaving Ronald to run it alone. Steve would come out and speak to the youth and give seminars with Ronald when he had the opportunity.

On The Road Again

Ronald got a call from another city for him and Mervyn to come and speak to their school and a workshop for 20 officers, some that specialized in gangs, others were Police Chiefs of those cities along with Lt Gov. John Wilder. Some reason the morning they needed to be there traffic was heavy and put them behind. Ronald asked Mervyn to call and inform them they were going to be late. The Chief told them not to worry about the speed limits. He said if any officers stopped them to have them to be notified. Mervyn looked at Ronald and he pushed the pedal to the medal. They drove 95mph, passing officers along the way down Highway 64 to Middleton in no time. Ronald talked to the students about choices and the consequences using his life as an example. Ronald and Mervyn laughed as they finished the workshop. They never would have thought as young gang bangers they would be speaking to officers of the law about helping troubled youths of today. Ronald and Mervyn saw it all too much when young people didn't listen. Ronald would either see them at Juvenile Court, in the hospital or visiting their gravesides. Some just didn't get the picture. Ronald would get this strange look from the young boys that were hard headed when they would see him at Juvenile Court. Ronald didn't like to show his badge much. It scared the people he was trying to reach. Some times mentoring a child would get next to him and make him cry. Some of the people children he was trying to help didn't live in the best of places, sometimes without food in the house. He would go get food for the family and spend as much time with that young man as possible.

Ronald's life didn't change much from day to day; wake up, thank God, shower, put his clothes on, check his voice mail messages, check his emails and out the door rolling to his car to speak at a school about gangs, drugs, teen violence, AIDS, and teen pregnancy, and parenting. He'd leave there and go to a school to mentor children. On too many occasions nurses that took care of Ronald and Mervyn would have them come up and speak to those that had been paralyzed at The Med. Ronald realized that if children didn't get an education they were going to be lost to a destination of wheelchairs, graveyards, and jail cells. He also knew jobs needed to be made for those that needed jobs. A lot of the teens

Ronald spoke with were angry at their conditions; hungry with no food, no clothes for school, lights off and they felt trapped, abandoned by parents, given up on with no hope left to survive the best way they can even if that meant robbing, selling drugs, stealing, selling their bodies to feed themselves and to survive. Ronald understood their feelings. He had been there. Having those feelings brought back memories of a strong mother doing what she had to do to survive for her and her children. Ronald had to remind them of hope and the fact they had to believe in themselves and Jesus in spite of what people may say.

You've heard those words before that cut deeper than a knife and hurt to the bone. When you hear words like you'll never be anything in life, you are just like your father or mother; they can kill a person's spirit to have motivation, a drive, and passion for something in life. Ronald was blessed to have seen, traveled, and told his life story. He had spoken in places he never would have imagined ever visiting. On many occasions students would pull up a chair and talk to him about their problems. Some were involved in gangs and wanted to get out. Ronald would help them if they were serious about getting out. No real gang member wants his or her child forced into a gang, it's a choice. That was the code in their laws and policies.

Every chance Ronald got to help single mothers with a young son he would talk to the mother and see if she would do her part. He saw too many of single parents looking for mentors for their sons and daughters, instead of getting involved in their children lives. They forgot that is what a parent is supposed to do. A lot of single parents wanted to pass off the responsibility of raising a child after having too many or they wanted to live their own lives. He saw too many times single mothers and single fathers willing to allow the person they were seeing not participate in their children lives at all and couldn't understand why they would lay down and give themselves to people who didn't love them enough to be a part of their child's life.

Handicapped? Who Said?

Ronald would get calls from parents who had a son they wanted talked to because he didn't take out the garbage. Ronald had to remind the parents that once they were teens and they made mistakes also. He would tell these parents to use their lives as a means to reach their children simply by sitting down and talking to their children. It helps the children see their parents in a realistic light instead as always demanding of the child. Mervyn would get calls from mothers to talk to their children about similar matters; same stories, different faces. Ronald, Mervyn, and Darryl would get together as much as they could to clear their heads. Sometimes they would be in different places. Mervyn would be out in San Diego calling Ronald while he was in Austin and Darryl would be in Illinois, but when they were together they'd get together to hit a favorite spot out of town from time to time.

Every now and then Ronald would help single mothers with daughters. Another problem was starting to be brought into the factor; GTO's (gay girls taking over). One afternoon Ronald was lying on the couch watching the news when he got a phone call. It was a grandmother who needed his help with her granddaughter. It seems these girls at school had picked her granddaughter out because the leader liked her. Every day the leader of the GTO's would send her girls from their click to pick on the granddaughter until she got tired and joined them. They figured because the grandmother was old and had some health problems she wouldn't be help for her granddaughter. God blesses us with gifts to help others. However, sometimes we use those gifts to hurt rather than help. Ronald learned that people choose the method in which they want to use the gift but fail to realize the consequences of their choices. Ronald could go out and mislead hundreds of teens but would that help them? Ronald decided he'd talk to the young lady and help her. He found out who the girls were, their names, where they hung out at and their ages. After that, he talked to his associates that assist him. Ronald figured it would be best to talk to the leader of the group and see if they would leave the young lady alone before taking steps to go to school and police department. The leader of the group agreed to leave the girl alone after that conversation.

It was nice outside that morning when Ronald got a call from prison. His friend told him horrible stories about young boys18,19, 20 years of age weighing about a hundred pounds soaking wet waiting for it to rain while in prison. They would go out on the yard looking up to the sky and cry as the rain would cover their faces and hide the tears they shed over the choices that they had made. They thought they were killers until they faced men without a gun. One of Ronald teacher's that was the girls coach at Westside High School at one time asked him he would come over and speak to her students. This was an opportunity he had always wanted, so he told her yes. She told him what day and time to be there. On the day of the speaking engagement he was told by her several gang members were coming up to the school and get him. Ronald rolled on into the school and said, "let them come". Ronald and others that worked as mentors to single mothers of sons in the community were trying to save the very sons and daughters of those men and women that are gang members in prisons. Consequently, the lives of Ronald and his associates were threatened from time to time. He would have conversation with his associates and he would ask them where is the church?

Ronald was talking to former gang members, police officers, pastors and others. When he was an active gang member he believed in what he was doing and would have died because he believed what he read from the laws and policies as a gangster disciples. Ronald thought with as much money coming into the churches why weren't there scholarships for their members' children, mentors for single mothers' sons in each church. Where were the masses of pastors? As many as there were, why didn't the big churches help the small churches to build the youth up in the small churches or come together and set a side a sum from each church with independent people over seeing the funds to start educational programs for the children in the community?

He Didn't Have To Do It

Ronald continued to think about the commitment of Christians. Do gang members believe more in what they are doing than the people that say they are Christians in churches today? That made what a Caucasian police officer did for him so meaningful. That a police officer would step outside himself, his surrounding, his boundaries and help a young African American gangbanger. He did and because of a mentor like Steve, Ronald wanted to save other young boys out there. Several months later Ronald was asked to come back over to Westside High School and speak again. He said no problem and asked when and what time. When he arrived, they took him to the gym full of young boys; about 300 hundred with hopes, goals, and dreams ahead of them. He started talking about his life as the young men listened and hoped they would take heed and make better choices that included staying away from drugs, teen violence, gangs, AIDS, and teen pregnancies. A week later, Ronald learned that six students tried to jump in a 15-year-old boy into G-Unit gang in the bathroom and killed him.

Ronald sat there shaking his head in his home in disbelief. A life of possibilities and aspirations had been taken away from a mother. Ronald realized while their parents were being slaying in the spirit at church, which is not biblically sound. Their children were just being slain.

MEMPHIS GANGS

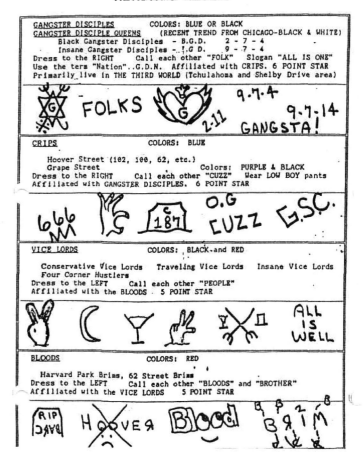

GANGSTER DISCIPLES   COLORS: BLUE OR BLACK
GANGSTER DISCIPLE QUEENS   (RECENT TREND FROM CHICAGO-BLACK & WHITE)
    Black Gangster Disciples - B.G.D.   2 - 7 - 4
    Insane Gangster Disciples - I.G D.   9 - 7 - 4
Dress to the RIGHT   Call each other "FOLK"   Slogan "ALL IS ONE"
Use the term "Nation"..G.D.N. Affiliated with CRIPS. 6 POINT STAR
Primarily live in THE THIRD WORLD (Tchulahoma and Shelby Drive area)

CRIPS   COLORS: BLUE

    Hoover Street (102, 100, 62, etc.)
    Grape Street   Colors: PURPLE & BLACK
Dress to the RIGHT   Call each other "CUZZ"   Wear LOW BOY pants
Affiliated with GANGSTER DISCIPLES. 6 POINT STAR

VICE LORDS   COLORS: BLACK and RED

    Conservative Vice Lords   Traveling Vice Lords   Insane Vice Lords
    Four Corner Hustlers
Dress to the LEFT   Call each other "PEOPLE"
Affiliated with the BLOODS . 5 POINT STAR

BLOODS   COLORS: RED

    Harvard Park Brims, 62 Street Brims
Dress to the LEFT   Call each other "BLOODS" and "BROTHER"
Affiliated with the VICE LORDS   5 POINT STAR

Ronald started to hear gangs getting the blame for everything that happened in the neighborhoods, but every crime was not gang related. It was more out there to deceive, or trap, young people other than gangs and gang signs. Ronald was speaking at Stafford Academy where a good

137

friend, Dr. Jeffrey Taylor, worked. Dr. Taylor had recently become the president of P.I.A.N.O. Inc. Ronald got the chance to meet most of the staff there and the principal was a wise man. Ronald came to respect that principal very much because he saw how he and his staff were committed to helping the students. The staff at that school came up with interesting ways to get the students to think out side the box, to become creative in ways of using the students' talents and skills. Ronald often heard from boys at school how older men were using them and making them join gangs, forcing them to take drug and gun charges as they lied to them about how the crimes will not be affecting them because they were juveniles.

Ronald was trying to make sure the wannabe's stopped committing crimes and false flagging as a gang member. Many times Ronald and Mervyn would partner with other organizations that mentored children and were grass root organizations. Many of them didn't have a building for the teens to come to or the big budgets to assist those they served but they had changed and made a difference in many young people lives by getting them out of gangs, assisting them with jobs and clothes or their baby children if they had any. Ronald often wondered what would happen if they had the funds to use to reach the teens they worked with. Ronald had learned over time that the African Americans that lived in America were blessed because they could have been born in Kenya, Somalia, or Dar Fur. Why do we spend every dime we earn, he would wonder. Parents need to start thinking outside of the box. We have got to stop blaming other people when we have control over our finances. If we could come together as a people, imagine the possibilities.

Choices

Ronald would have to endure a great deal of things along the way while trying to assist young boys from trouble, pain, including the loss of friends and family. From time to time, Ronald would take trips to clear his head. Ronald drove his car while thinking about what had transpired at Westside. He started laughing as he thought about when Steve and he had spoken together on the radio station RBC Ministries on "Words To Live By" in Grands Rapids, Michigan. Ronald reflected on how far he had come and the things he had been blessed to do. To have had his life story told on over 475 stations world wide in Countries like Canada, the Caribbean, the Far East (Singapore, Philippians, and Korea), Central America (Nicaragua and Guatemala) and Africa (South Africa and Nigeria).

Then something unexpected happened. Ronald got a call from his cousin Toe. Toe's son had been shot and was in the hospital. Ronald couldn't believe what he was hearing. The same little boy he had once held in his hands as a baby laid there in the TICU at The Med. He was paralyzed from the neck down and had complications from a cowardly act of a shooting that he had no part of. Ronald went in and started talking to his cousin about the road ahead. His little cousin wanted to know how he survived his injury, pain, muscle spasms, and bedsores along with other things. Ronald took a deep breath before he said Jesus; Ronald replied he prayed a lot. It hurt even more when Ronald saw his little cousin suffering, hurting from pain to nerves , and ligaments that he knew would take a long time to heal and he couldn't help him. Ronald left the hospital and went to his place to think. The words he would tell young people kept playing over and over in his head "jail cells, grave yards, and wheelchairs" living the life style he has lived will put you in one of these positions but the choice is yours to make and there are consequences to that choice whether right or wrong.

One evening in July of 2004, Ronald was hanging out at a restaurant on Beale Street when he heard a soft voice asked him if he comes there often. The voice
also asked and what the six-point star on his wrist represented. Ronald had no idea who it was talking to him. He turned around and there she stood; a lovely woman smiling at him. She introduced herself as Wendi, the assistant editor for The Commercial Appeal in Memphis. She asked if she could interview him about his life and he agreed to the interview. She believed his life story would be very interesting to tell; a black young gang banger who hated two types of people for all the wrong reasons and how God showed him his loving plan for him in spite of some pain and suffering. They agreed to meet with the others that played a part in life.

Wendi met Ronald's brother Darryl; a friend Mervyn, who was a former Vice lord and also in a wheelchair from a gunshot to the neck; Denzil, another friend that helped mentor at risk boys; one of the young boys under Ronald's supervision as a probation officer; and of course Steve, the white police officer who saved Ronald's life in more ways than one. Wendi talked to everyone and they agreed to meet at a restaurant downtown and take pictures along with the interview. The title of the article was *Could a God Love Me?* She began with questions about the choices Ronald had made. Ronald had chose , like many young teens, to live a fast, hard life. This choice involved selling weed and cocaine, skipping school, stealing, shooting, fighting, smoking weed, and drinking. When he was 17, a security guard shot him during a failed
robbery attempt in Frayser. Paralyzed from the waist down, he spent two

months at the Regional Medical Center in Memphis. Mad at the world and himself, spitting at his nurses, he didn't think there was a life after being shot and living in a wheelchair. God saw otherwise. Ronald, now 37, found a life as a volunteer with Juvenile Court and with his attempts to help single mothers (like his) and fatherless kids (like him). His transformation came, in part, through an unlikely source: a white cop, Steve Grisham. Steve won't take any credit for how Ronald's life has changed. Long before Ronald chose to rob, steal, and try to kill, Steve says, God had chosen Ronald first. Much of Ronald's story is what you'd expect; a kid doing the wrong thing with the wrong people. His mom spent much time patrolling the streets on foot looking for her two sons hoping they were not dead, but it wasn't enough. Ronald joined the Night Hawks and the Gangster Disciples at 14. He said they spent as much time singing and dancing, as thugging. As the money grew, the violence grew and they had to protect themselves. The violence led to unfortunate situations, but God's grace proved as always to be more than sufficient.

1. Bobby and Denise left Juvenile Court and Kathy and Mammie came Ronald didn't know how they would see him there. One day Ronald got an invitation in the mail from Commercial Appeal papers asking him to come to the Peabody Hotel on this day and time. Ronald agreed to go and when he got there, Ronald, his brother Darryl, and Phillip a brother from another mother. He saw Kathy and Mammie. Ronald was surprised to see Mammie, Lilly, Kathy, Jerry, Chief Brown and his beautiful wife Pat all there at the award show.

2.

Ronald was the 2005 recipient of the prestigious Jefferson Award for his service with Juvenile Court, the City of Memphis and Shelby County.

2

They wanted to show him how much they appreciated him on that night for his service. Next week a picture of him with the words of why he was nominated were mounted and hangs in Juvenile Court wall of Jefferson Awards in the Lobby to this very day.

Congratulations -
RONALD BALDRIDGE
2005 Jefferson Award Winner

2007.01.13.18:51:13

Ronald, Mervyn and Darryl had just come back from taking a trip to the south coast and relaxing for a while. When he and , the members of his company got an invitation to come on the first black radio station in Memphis and the country WDIA. That was just one of the reasons this radio station had lasted so long because they had out of the box thinkers as radio personalities. Bev Johnson was one of those out of the box thinkers. She thought since gangs and teen crimes in the schools and the community were on the rise. She had them on to talk and answer questions about gangs and what to look for as well as methods to use to build a better relationship with their children.

Ronald Baldridge has truly learned that life is about choices. It doesn't matter if you are born black or white, rich or poor, urban or rural. Life is about taking what you have in front of you and making the right choices to mold your resources into your dream. What about you young boy or

143

young girl, sir or maam? What will your choices be? What do you have to work with? Are you satisfied with where your life is? Are you comfortable with where your life is going? Who knows what lives you can touch or change to affect for the good of mankind? It wasn't because he was black, or grew up poor, or live in North Memphis. It was the choices he made. Ronald was able to turn his life around. The consequences of bad decisions in the past made Ronald painfully aware of the changes he needed to make. Ronald chose to make that choice. Again, what will your choices be? Ronald knows now that the lifestyle he previously lived always ends one of three ways: wheel chairs, graveyard, or, jail cells. Ronald has experienced all three of these consequences. What will your choices be? To this very day Ronald works with at risk young boys of single mothers before they end up in wheelchairs, graveyards, jail cells and after they are in wheelchairs .

Super Model Iman & Ronald Baldridge

Ronald
congratulated by Tom Joyner Morning Sky Show,

County
Mayor of Memphis Mayor AC Wharton and Mrs. Wharton his lovely wife
and Ronald Keynote speaker @ a Middle school graduation,

145

Donna Joyner
(Tom Joyner's wife) and Ronald Baldridge with two other fans in Memphis.

Ronald, Susan Taylor, and Mervyn of P.I.A.N.O. Inc. (in wheelchairs) at Memphis Cares Mentoring Launch at The Dr. Martin L. King Civil Rights Museum

A Poem dedicated to Earline Baldridge
"What A Woman That's A Mother"

146

Strong, Petite, Black And The Most Beautiful Mother Formed. When I Was Sick, Hurting, Afraid, And In Doubt Because Of God's Blessing He Created You.

It Was To You I Came To Help Me Weather The Storms...

Giving Me Hugs, Up @all Times Of Night Watching Over Us Killing Bugs.

Caring, Concern, Working, Coming Home To Two Hard Headed Boys Cooking Meals, Helping With Homework, Teaching Us How To Cook, Clean And Survive.

A Mother Doing What She Has To Do To Keep Her And Two Sons Alive...

Yes Sexy, Sensual, The Quintessential Of A Woman That's A Mother Running The Race...It's Hard Not Hearing Her Voice And Seeing Her Beautiful Face...

Look At Her Men You Desire To Touch, Please Don't Mess With Her Sons Or Call Her The Wrong Name... Your Words Are Futile Keep The Game... You'll Get Cut By Her Or Hurt, Out Of All These Things She Is And More... She's What A Woman That's A Mother For Sure...

By Ronald Baldridge

P.IAN.O. INC.
EIN NUMBER 65-1270345

Bringing harmony back into the lives of at risk boys by working together like keys on a piano.

*Mission Statement: **P.I.A.N.O.** is a 501© 3 non-profit organization that's tax deductible. We reach out to at risk boy's age's 10- 17 years old of single mothers. P.I.A.N.O. INC. mission is bringing harmony back into the lives of at* *risk boys by working together like keys on a piano. We can accomplish this through partnering with business sector, corporations and public sector. Speaking to and working with as many single mothers sons in the Churches, Juvenile facilities throughout the city, hospitals, Memphis City and county schools. Mentoring and assisting in finding the right positive male role model for that young boy, as well as having creative thinking and rap sessions using common methods to assist them toward their future success. Helping them understand the importance of making moral and positive choices in the most difficult time of decision-making. To help them understand the consequences of choices, in doing so*

Gangs –
Parents Guide A Parent's Guide for Preventing Gangs Many communities (maybe the one you live in) have serious problems with gangs. There are many kinds of gangs, but whatever kind you community is dealing with, gangs spell trouble. They cause fear, destroy property, threaten or hurt p peaceable residents, and drive out businesses.

Parents can do a lot to prevent gang problems or to help reduce gang problems already

In place. Most important, there's a lot that parents can do to keep

your own children from joining gangs:

- Learn about gangs and signs of gang activity.

- Sharpen your skills as a parent and use them.

Join with others to make or keep your neighborhood gang free. These are especially important:

- Talk with and listen to your child. Spend some special time with each child.,

- Put a high value on education and help your child to do his or her best in

school. Do everything possible to prevent dropping out,

- Help your kids identify positive role models and heroes - especially

Do everything possible to involve your children in supervised, positive group activities.,

- Praise them for doing well and encourage them
to do their very best - to

stretch their skills to the utmost,

- Know what your children are doing and whom
they are with. Know about their friends and their
friends' families.,

Don't forget to talk about gangs. The best time is before there's a major

problem. Tell your child that

- you disapprove of gangs,

- you don't want to see your child hurt or arrested, - you see your child as special,
and worth
protecting, - you want to help your child with prob
lems,- family members don't keep secrets from
each other, and - you an other parents are working
together against gangs. Don't forget to listen to your
child as well

II

LEARN ABOUT GANGS

Young people (as young as nine or ten) join gangs for reasons that makes sense

to them, if not to adults. They give reasons like these: -to belong to a group,

- for excitement,

- to get protection,

- to earn money, and

- to be with friends.

Gangs leave signs of their presence. Your child may adopt some of those signs as

either a gang member or an imitator: \

- specific colors or emblems,

- special hand signals,,

worse grades,, staying out without good reason,,

- "hanging" with known or suspected gang members, or, carrying weapons.,- wearing certain kinds and colors of clothing in very specific ways, and , possessing unexplained, relatively large sums of money.,

Many gang members say they joined because the gang offered them support, caring, and a sense of order and purpose - all the things that most parents miss . Try to give their kids.

The odds are that the better you meet these needs, the less need your children will see for gangs. Contact police department and other non-profit organization to find mentors.

ACCOMPLISHMENTS: P.I.A.N.O. Inc. Have in the past partnered with educators, politicians, law enforcement agencies, doctors, teens, churches and several Memphis City and County schools. We've spoken to crowds of 2 to 2,000 people at one time. P.I.A.N.O. Inc. has spoken in Grand Rapids Michigan *Words To Live By*, (June 2000). Members of P.I.A.N.O. Inc. have spoken on various radio stations AM 640-WCRV (2000), AM 990-*The Light* (1996), K-97-*On Point* a talk show (2003), FM 101.1 (1998). Mr. Peters and I have appeared at the Red Ribbon Festival, in Middleton, Tennessee with Lt. Gov. John Wilder and Chief of Police Monroe Jordan (November 2004). Spoke to Youth for Christ (November 2004).

We have facilitated youth conferences; Bridges, Memphis, TN (February 2006), Youth Villages, Arlington, TN (June 2002), The Regional Medical Center spinal cord peer counseling (1988-2000), and the Y-DAC youth detention facilities (February 2002).

The television station WREG-Channel 3 produced a 30-minute special about me called "Beating The Odds" (April 1996). Ronald was featured in a front-page newspaper article for the Commercial Appeal by Wendy C. Thomas, "Could A God Love Me" (August 2004), *featured in a front –page newspaper article Tri-State Defender by Wiley Henry, "Redemption" (May 27-31,2006), featured in Proud Magazine* "From A Gang to God"(December 2005), and the *Spirit of Memphis* magazine "A Wonderful Change" by Katrena Mitchell (October 2005) and my life story has been told in over 10 countries.

Ronald was the recipient of numerous awards from Juvenile Court (1999-2005),

K-97 radio *Peace Achiever of the Month for March* (2003), FM Hot 107(1997), *The Tom Joyner Morning Show*, "Real Father Real Men" contest (June 2001), and the prestigious Nobel Prize called *The Jefferson Award*

151

created by Jacqueline Kennedy Onasis, former Senator Robert Taft, Jr., and Sam Beard of the Commercial Appeal (April 14,2005). Ronald has lived in a wheelchair for 24 years. Since that time he was shot 5 different times, thrown 3 feet out a car while car was going 45mph , 24 different operations, broken right leg , dislocated right hip, broken left hand and left ankle Ronald

For more information or speaking engagements please call.

P.I.A.N.O. INC.

Chief Executive Administrator

Ronald Baldridge

Motivational Speaker• Anti-Gang Consultants • Spinal cord Peer Counselor

Recipient of the prestigious Nobel Prize Jefferson Award, by Jacqueline Kennedy Onasis

Office: 901.649.8585 • Fax: 901.525.9145 • baldridgerb@aol.com .

Website:http://hometown.aol.com/baldridgerb/PIANOINCindex.html

Continued from page B1

STUDENTS

Juvenile Court.

The fighting attracted media attention and has been mentioned by school district and community leaders who have unveiled a number of initiatives in recent weeks aimed at reducing school violence.

The peace rally, titled "Stop the Violence, Increase the Peace," brought community leaders, police officers and a sheriff's deputy to address several dozen students assembled in the gym.

Ladies' Club members, wearing pink shirts and khaki pants, served popcorn and other snacks on the sidelines as parents, staff and students — including the school's entire football team — listened intently.

Sgt. Richard Almond of the Shelby County Sheriff's Office told students safer schools start with them.

He applauded the student-led effort to create the peace rally and asked students to report criminal activity to the school administration or to local law enforcement.

"If you know something is going on, don't feel like you are snitching on someone by going to an administrator. It is the right thing to do," Almond said.

He also explained the new Trust Pays program, a program Crime Stoppers has instituted in partnership with Memphis City and Shelby County Schools.

Ronald Baldridge, a former drug dealer who now runs a nonprofit agency for at-risk black boys, shared his story with students and urged them not to make the same mistakes he did.

Baldridge has been confined to a wheelchair since he was shot in the spine during a robbery he and a friend committed 22 years ago.

"Life is about choices," he told students. "Figure out what you want to do with your life and start making those choices now."

Sophomore Anita Bateman said she found the program uplifting.

Kayla Stegall, also a 10th grader, said she hoped her fellow students took heed of the lessons offered by the speakers.

"I thought (Baldridge) inspired us the most," she said. "He gave us a story we can connect with."

— Dakarai I. Aarons: 529-65

153